Marco Pierre White in
Hell's Kitchen

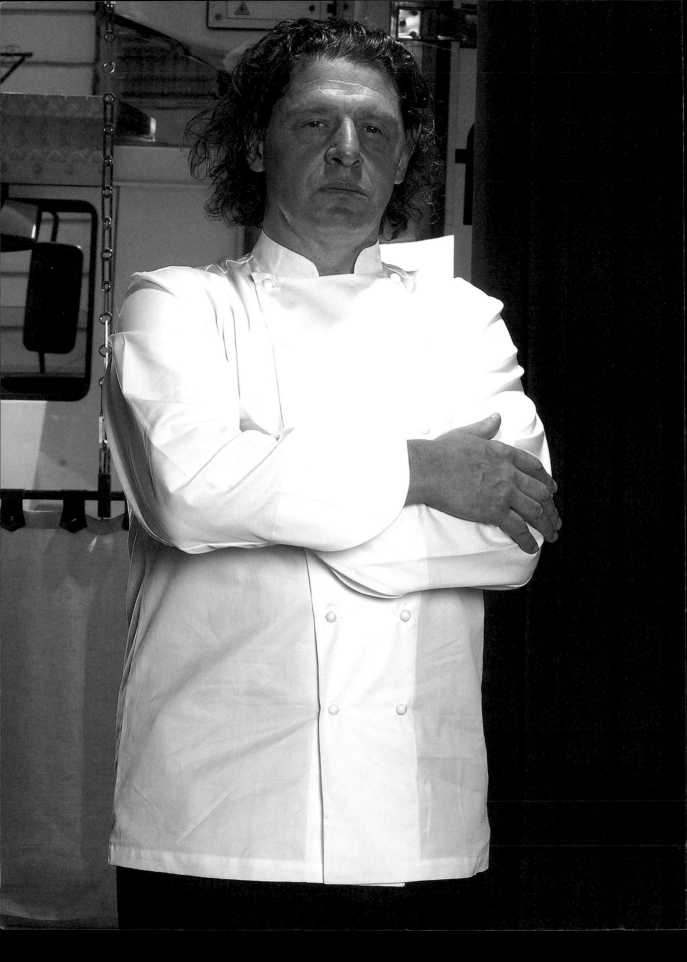

Marco Pierre White in
Hell's Kitchen

EBURY
PRESS

ITV Productions Limited

To Luciano, Marco and Mirabelle, the 3 stars that really shine.

1 3 5 7 9 10 8 6 4 2

Published in 2007 by Ebury Press, an imprint of Ebury Publishing

A Random House Group Company

Text © 2007 ITV Productions Limited

Marco Pierre White has asserted his right to be identified as the author of this Work in accordance with the Copyright, Designs and Patents Act 1988

The Random House Group Limited Reg. No. 954009

Addresses for companies within the Random House Group can be found at www.randomhouse.co.uk

A CIP catalogue record for this book is available from the British Library

The Random House Group Limited makes every effort to ensure that the papers used in our books are made from trees that have been legally sourced from well-managed and credibly certified forests. Our paper procurement policy can be found on www.randomhouse.co.uk

To buy books by your favourite authors and register for offers visit www.rbooks.co.uk

Co-writer Alexandra Antonioni
Editor Norma MacMillan
Designer Tony Lyons
Photographers Sian Irvine, Norman Hollands and William Lingwood (food) and Dave Bentley (reportage and portraits)

Printed and bound in Germany by APPL Druck, Wemding

ISBN 9780091923167

Contents

Foreword

I have been condemned many times in my life for being controversial, though I've never thought of myself as such because I have always put foundation behind my statements. Maybe my 'methods' could be construed as being controversial but if you open up the Michelin Guide today, it proves they worked. Most of my reputation is a product of exaggeration and ignorance.

I couldn't live a lie or stray from my stove, which is why on 23 December 1999 I hung up my apron for what I thought was the last time. However, like great boxers, we all have one last fight left within us. That 'want' to step into the ring one last time is the only way I can explain my feelings. To risk everything that I have ever worked for and everything I have ever stood for is lunacy, but let's not forget that for me stepping back into the kitchen is stepping back into a world that I feel very comfortable in – indeed, it is the world, the environment that I grew up in.

Some of the programmes I see on television do not give a true insight into how a kitchen is run. They don't show you the love, the romance, the true story. This is my reason for stepping back into the ring, putting my apron back on, maybe for the very last time. I feel I have a duty, not just to my industry, but also to my children and to myself. When you've been put down as many times as I have you get to like the smell of the canvas.

The world that I walked into was Escoffier's world, the tail end of that world. As a boy I put my career into the hands of many great chefs. I never asked them how many hours I would have to work or how much I would be paid. I was there for the knowledge, the experience, the philosophy and the privilege to cook with those heavyweights. Let's never forget the bollockings they gave me, because without all those bollockings I would never have been the cook I became. As my first-ever boss, Colin Long of the Box Tree, said, 'Never forget, Marco, it's better to be s**t upon than to be ignored'. You see, in a strange sort of way it's a form of affection. It's never personal. Service is service, we have a job to do, a duty to our customers and a reputation to defend and uphold. One of the things I love about my industry is that it accepts everybody from every background, without ever asking too many questions.

If we are really honest we are in the business of selling fun — a night out. Food and wine are a by-product of what we do. To take food too seriously is to take yourself too seriously. Unfortunately most young chefs are fuelled and ruled by their insecurity. Let's not forget that success is born out of arrogance. Most cooks when they are young tend to overwork their food to hide their lack of confidence and appreciation for Mother Nature. In time they learn that she is the true artist — we're just the cooks. There's nothing better than to watch a young chef develop and his confidence grow. It always shows on the plate.

It was Fernand Point of the celebrated restaurant Les Pyramides in Vienne who once said: 'Perfection is lots of little things done well.' I didn't ever meet Fernand but his book *Ma Gastronomie* is the only book I have ever read from cover to cover more than once. This was the man who invented La Cuisine Nouvelle, which was derived from classical French cuisine but 'lightened'. It is as my mother always told me: 'A tree without roots is a piece of wood.' Thus every cook needs a solid foundation and to learn to respect the classics.

I was a boy who saw the tail end of the 'old world', hence I'm old school. Maybe today I'm out of date, but that's fine. Every ship needs an anchor and I'm happy to be that anchor to my industry. When I was a boy there was no such thing as the 'celebrity chef'. You went to work to learn your trade and do your job. The industry I stepped into all those years ago was a special world

– and still is in many ways. The thing I disapprove of in modern gastronomy is the politics. The hotel and restaurant world is a very large jigsaw made up of many pieces and many people doing a myriad of jobs. We need to respect them all because without each and every piece it would be a very boring world indeed.

For me the true golden age of gastronomy has gone. It's a different world now, full of different people with different values. There are too many awards and too many chefs wanting to be celebrities. I say be famous for being behind your stove and for what you put on the plate. Only a fool strays from his stove. If you no longer want to be there then pluck up the courage to let go of your status and give back your stars. No chef is happy to live a lie and by letting go you will have the time and energy to be kinder to yourself, to discover yourself. It is only by growing to know yourself that you do things for the right reasons and maybe have a chance to be really happy and realise your true potential as a person. Being at that high level in the world of gastronomy you become emotionally stunted and socially inept, which is understandable as all of your energy and creativity goes into your food.

Cooking should be a way of life – an extension of oneself – never a job.

Marco Pierre White

London, 2007

Great chefs
are born out of
insecurity.
Great food is born
out of love.

Chef's note

When cooking I don't always season with salt, especially when it comes to meat. Instead I like to season using chicken stock cubes (Knorr is my preference). I add a pinch or two when cooking all meat sauces and gravies and also when making vegetable soups. Firstly, this is more forgiving than salt and, secondly, when finishing sauces you don't have to reduce them so much to reach their desired flavour. This makes the finished product lighter rather than over-reduced and over-strong in natural salt.

When cooking vegetables, a crumbled cube in the water vastly improves their flavour. Another great use is when roasting a chicken: create a light paste using chicken stock cubes and some olive oil, then spread this over the breast of the chicken and inside the cavity walls of the bird, rather than seasoning with lots of salt.

Too many chefs turn their noses up at certain products, but when you think about it a burger is not a burger without ketchup; an English breakfast is not a breakfast without HP sauce; fish 'n' chips are not the same without malt vinegar; and that great British institution the ham sandwich is not a proper ham sandwich without English mustard.

Let's not forget that good food is all about flavour and the home cook should never be afraid to use these products. Dry good stores in many acclaimed restaurants have all these ingredients and more in them and chefs use them freely and without compunction.

Good eating.

Painting by numbers is one thing but cooking by them is something else.

Chapter One
Soups

Chilled Tomato Soup
Gazpacho andalouse

The perfect soup for a summer's day. It combines all the flavours of the Mediterranean whilst being extremely easy to prepare. You can add whatever takes your fancy, maybe some croûtons or a little pesto, or you can make it even more interesting by adding some freshly cooked seafood such as lobster, langoustines or a little white crab meat.

700 g plum tomatoes, skinned and seeded
$1/_2$ cucumber, peeled and seeded
$1/_2$ onion, finely chopped
3 garlic cloves, finely chopped
5 red peppers, seeded and chopped
75 ml sherry vinegar
2 tbsp Mayonnaise (page 148)
Tabasco sauce
sea salt and freshly ground black pepper

1. Liquidize the first six ingredients until smooth, then pass through a fine sieve. Season well with a little salt and pepper, whisk in the mayonnaise and add Tabasco to suit your personal taste.

2. Serve well chilled.

Tip > The most important thing to remember is to insure that the tomatoes are of the very best quality and erring on being just a little too ripe.

Curried Mussel Soup
Soupe de moules Billy-by

The brick-red colour of this soup is simply stunning. The two main ingredients, namely mussels and saffron, complement each other beautifully to give a really concentrated burst of flavour. This is so important in a starter, where we are looking for something to stimulate the palate without ruining our appetite with anything overly rich or heavy. Once again you can be adventurous with the garnishes. One idea, if you don't want to use oysters as is done here, is to add some diced potato and a few snipped chives, or maybe simply croûtons sprinkled with a few extra strands of saffron.

2 kg fresh mussels

1 onion, finely chopped

1 celery stick, finely chopped

1 white part of leek, finely chopped

25 g unsalted butter

1 tsp curry powder

pinch of saffron strands

$^1/_2$ tsp cayenne pepper

sprig of thyme

1 bay leaf

600 ml white wine

300 ml Fish Stock (page 139)

450 ml double cream

sea salt

Garnish

4 Native oysters, No. 2

1. Wash the mussels and pull off their beards, then wash them again carefully.

2. Sweat the vegetables gently in the butter for 5 minutes. Add the curry powder, saffron strands, cayenne and herbs, then add the mussels. Continue to cook gently with the lid on for another minute. Add the wine and stock, and cook for another few minutes, still covered, until all the mussels are open.

3. Pick the mussels out of the pan and set aside. Strain the stock through muslin or a fine sieve into a clean pan. Bring to the boil and reduce the stock by half. Add the cream and reduce further until the soup is the consistency of thin cream. Season with a little salt if required (depending on the saltiness of the mussels this may not be needed).

4. To serve, remove the mussels from their shells and place a few in each soup bowl along with a freshly shucked oyster lying on the very bottom. Heat the soup to just below boiling point and pour over the mussels.

Tip > As ever, the golden rule when cooking mussels is to discard any that fail to close before you have cooked them and any that fail to open once you have.

Soup of Red Mullet with Saffron
Soupe de rouge au safran

The delicate flavour of red mullet coupled with saffron produces an earthy but truly refined fish soup. You should start making it the day before serving, to allow the mullet enough time to marinate. It is the garnishes that really make this into something out of the ordinary, so don't skimp on them. Put them on the table separately to allow others to add as much as they choose.

10 red mullets

100 ml olive oil

pinch of saffron strands

pinch of cayenne pepper

1 onion

$1/2$ head of celery

$1/2$ fennel bulb

$1/2$ bulb of garlic

250 g tomatoes, diced

450 g tomato purée

175 ml Pernod

175 ml Cognac

2 litres Fish Stock (page 139)

$1/2$ large potato, peeled and thinly sliced

Garnishes

Rouille (page 150)

Gruyère cheese, grated

small crisp croûtons

1. Scale the mullets and cut off the heads. Remove and discard the innards, plus the gills and the eyes. Wash all the pieces thoroughly in cold water. Cut up each body into three equal pieces. Place everything, heads and all, in a dish.

2. Mix the olive oil with the saffron and cayenne, and add to the fish. Rub the oil into the fish, then leave to marinate in the fridge for 24 hours.

3. Peel or trim the onion, celery, fennel and garlic, then cut into small dice (this is known as a *mirepoix*). Cook the *mirepoix* in a large saucepan in a little of the marinade oil until golden. Add the tomato dice and, when the liquid had disappeared, stir in the tomato purée. Cook gently for about 10 minutes.

4. Meanwhile, remove the mullet pieces from their marinade and pan fry, in batches, for a few minutes on each side until they are golden brown.

5. Pour the Pernod and Cognac into the *mirepoix* pan and set alight. When the flame has subsided, reduce until the alcohol has evaporated. Add the mullet pieces. Cover the fish and vegetables with the fish stock, adding a little water if needed. Add the potato. Simmer gently for $1\frac{1}{2}$ hours.

6. Remove from the heat and blend the whole thing (including fish bones) in a food processor until smooth – you may have to do this in batches. Pass through a very fine sieve up to six times for the finest texture.

7. Reheat gently, then serve in hot soup plates, with bowls of rouille, grated Gruyère and croûtons.

Tip > You really do need a first-rate fish stock as a base for this dish. I suggest you make the stock in advance and freeze if necessary until you make the soup.

Cream of Celery Soup with Chives
Velouté de céleri au ciboulette

Deceptively simple but tasting of extravagance, this is a lavish soup made using only very basic ingredients. You could serve this without the egg but it does add a certain richness and looks very pretty on the plate.

250 g celery, finely sliced

250 g celeriac, peeled and finely sliced

1 onion, finely sliced

1 white part of leek, finely sliced

50 g unsalted butter

100 g potatoes, peeled and finely sliced

500 ml double cream

500 ml Chicken Stock (page 138)

1 tsp white wine vinegar

4 very fresh eggs

salt and freshly ground white pepper

Garnish

finely snipped chives

1. Gently sweat the celery, celeriac, onion and leek in the butter, making sure they do not colour, until all the moisture has evaporated. Season with salt and pepper.

2. Place the raw potato slices in a separate pan with the cream and stock, and bring to the boil. Add the sweated vegetables. Cook on a high heat for 10 minutes. Liquidize until smooth, then pass through a fine sieve into a clean pan.

3. Bring a small pan of water to the boil. Add the vinegar and poach the eggs. Drain and keep warm.

4. To serve, reheat the soup to just below boiling point and warm the soup bowls. Place a poached egg in the centre of each bowl, ladle the hot soup over it and sprinkle with the snipped chives.

Tip > The celery should be as young as you can get it, crisp and pale green in colour, and it is important to use a good clear chicken stock as this is where the intensity of flavour comes from.

A Soup of Salt Cod, Cream and Leeks
Soupe de brandade

Salt cod is a truly magical ingredient that is very under-utilized in this country, probably because it is rather unattractive to look at. But with the simplest of cooking it transforms itself into a truly gastronomic indulgence, and is the ultimate comfort food. This dish is great as a starter or perhaps a light luncheon with some crusty bread and a salad.

450 g salt cod

50 ml olive oil

115 g potatoes, peeled and thinly sliced

225 g white of leeks, thinly sliced

finely grated zest of $^1/_2$ orange

sprig of thyme

600 ml Fish Stock (page 139)

300 ml double cream

1. Dice the salt cod and leave under cold running water for 24 hours. This gets rid of most of the salt.

2. Drain the salt cod, then sauté gently in hot olive oil until all of the water evaporates.

3. Add the potatoes and sauté for about 5 minutes until soft. Do not allow to colour. Add the leeks, orange zest and thyme, and sweat for a further 4 minutes.

4. Pour in the fish stock and 450 ml water and bring to the boil. Skim and cook for 10 minutes.

5. Liquidize until smooth, then push through a fine sieve three times. Be sure to get rid of all the tiny fish bones.

6. Add the cream, bring back to the boil and pass through a sieve once again. Serve hot.

The hotel and restaurant world is like the French Foreign Legion – it accepts everybody, whatever their past or background.

Chapter Two
Starters

Russian Blinis with Oscietra Caviar

Blinis au caviar

To feed someone caviar is to truly spoil them. This is a very impressive starter. Home-made blinis are a world away from the packaged ones and worth the effort. The batter should be made well in advance to give it time to rise.

250 g fromage blanc

handful of chives, finely snipped

handful of flatleaf parsley, finely chopped

50 g shallots, finely chopped

2 garlic cloves, finely chopped

250 ml double cream, whipped to soft peaks

Blinis

50 g buckwheat flour

30 g fresh yeast

500 ml full fat milk

250 g wholemeal flour

4 eggs, separated

pinch of sugar

pinch of salt

80 g unsalted butter

Garnish

125 g Oscietra caviar

sprigs of chervil and chives

1. Place the fromage blanc in a piece of muslin or a clean tea towel, secure with string and suspend over a bowl to drain for 24 hours.

2. Discard the drained-off liquid and put the fromage blanc in the bowl. Fold in the herbs, shallots and garlic, then fold in the whipped cream. Keep in the fridge until needed.

3. For the blinis, place the buckwheat flour, yeast and milk in a bowl, cover and set aside for 1 hour.

4. Add the wholemeal flour, egg yolks and sugar to the yeast mixture and stir to mix. Leave covered for a further 2 hours.

5. Whisk the egg whites with the salt until they form stiff peaks. Fold them very gently into the batter mixture.

6. Cook the blinis one at a time (they should be 4–5 cm in diameter) in a non-stick pan, using a little butter each time. Cook for a couple of minutes on each side until they are a light golden brown. As they are cooked, place on a wire rack to keep warm.

7. To serve, put a blini on each plate. Using two dessertspoons, shape the fromage blanc into *quenelles* (small oval mounds) and place one on the centre of each blini. Top each with an equal amount of caviar, a small sprig of chervil and a few chives.

Tip > Real caviar is eye-wateringly expensive, even in small quantities. If you really can't stretch to it you can of course use lumpfish roe or keta, although it won't be quite the same. Another alternative is to replace the caviar with smoked salmon.

Salad of Lobster, New Potatoes and Truffle

Salade d'homard aux pommes de terre au truffe

Serving lobster and truffle on the same plate? It is surely the perfect marriage of two of nature's most precious gifts to any cook. This is a plate of food that screams seduction or for when you want to impress – or for when you want to make sure you get your own way. I suggest you cook the potatoes the day before to give them a chance to marinate properly.

6 new potatoes
Chicken Stock (page 138) to cover
150 ml Vinaigrette (page 149)
Court-Bouillon for Seafood (page 143) to cover
1 x 500 g live lobster
salt and freshly ground white pepper

Garnish
8 thin slices black truffle
flaked sea salt (*fleur de sel*)
chervil leaves

1. Scrape the new potatoes until they are clean, then cook them in chicken stock until tender. Pour off the stock and replace it with enough vinaigrette just to cover. Leave to marinate overnight, turning occasionally.

2. Bring the court-bouillon to the boil. Drop in the lobster, then take the pan off the heat. Set aside for 30 minutes. Drain well.

3. Slice the marinated potatoes into thin discs (about 5 mm thick) and arrange in a circular pattern on a large white plate. Warm briefly under a pre-heated grill.

4. Remove the lobster meat from the claws, taking care to keep the meat in a piece. Remove the meat from the tail and slice into 1 cm medallions. Arrange the lobster on top of the potatoes.

5. Garnish the lobster with the slices of black truffle and sprinkle the plate with a little vinaigrette, sea salt and chervil.

Tip > *Fleur de sel* is untreated salt that is allowed to dry naturally. It is available in most supermarkets and certainly in the posh delis that seem to be springing up all over the country these days. It is a wonderful addition to any home cook's larder as it is less harsh than regular sea salt and looks great on the plate.

Club Sandwich of Crab and Tomato
Tian de crabe et tomate, vinaigrette tomate

I love the clever use of tomato in this dish – as the foundation for the sandwich – creating an innovative and imaginative hors d'oeuvre. The combinations of flavours can be varied – you could perhaps use lobster instead of crab, for example. Whilst the sauces can be prepared well in advance the assembly needs to be fairly last-minute. As ever, the quality of ingredients is paramount here. This dish was created at 'The Restaurant, Marco Pierre White' by Robert Reid.

20 even-sized Dutch tomatoes, skinned

1 round lettuce

1 bunch watercress, leaves separated

25 ml Vinaigrette (page 149)

2 Golden Delicious apples

1 avocado

juice of 1 lemon

225 g fresh white crab meat

3 tbsp Mayonnaise (page 148)

Garnish
120 ml Tomato Coulis (page 152)
8 chervil leaves

1. Cut a thin slice off the stem end of each tomato and place them cut side down on the work surface. Cut a slice off each side of the tomato, scoop out the seeds and flesh, and flatten the tomato so that it forms a rectangle. You should end up with 20 rectangles, which will form the layers of the sandwiches. Be sure they are uniform and if necessary tidy with a sharp knife.

2. Separate the lettuce leaves. Take several leaves at a time, roll into a cigar shape and slice very thinly on the horizontal using a very sharp knife, to give you fine ribbons (*chiffonade*). Do the same with the watercress leaves. Keep the lettuce and watercress separate, and dress each with a small amount of vinaigrette.

3. Peel and core the apples, then cut into a 3 mm dice. Peel, stone and dice the avocado similarly. Keep separate and sprinkle both as quickly as you can with lemon juice to prevent discoloration (oxidization).

4. Shred the crab meat and mix with the mayonnaise and shredded lettuce. In a separate bowl combine the watercress, chopped apple and avocado.

5. Use four tomato rectangles for each sandwich. Lay the base tomato rectangles on a board side by side. Place a little of the lettuce and crab mixture on each rectangle and top with another tomato rectangle. Top this with more lettuce and crab, and then another tomato rectangle. Cover with the watercress, apple and avocado mixture. Finish off with a final layer of tomato.

6. Using a very sharp knife, cut down at an angle on both ends of the layered rectangle to transform it into a diamond.

7. Place a small amount of tomato coulis in the middle of each plate. Place a club sandwich in the centre and garnish with a chervil leaf at each end.

Tip > If you're not very confident in your knife work, you could also use a very sharp circular cutter to shape the club sandwich, which will look just as pretty.

Poached Oysters, Scrambled Egg and Caviar

Œufs brouillés au huîtres pochées, beurre blanc

Another incredible combination – oysters and caviar. Lightly poaching the oysters in their juices intensifies their natural 'sea flavour', which in turn is tempered by the creaminess of the eggs.

5 oysters, preferably Natives No. 2

50 ml Velouté for Fish (page 159)

lemon juice

15 g unsalted butter

2 eggs, beaten

1 tsp double cream

salt and freshly ground white pepper

Garnish

2 tsp caviar

sprigs of chervil

1. Open the oysters, keeping all their juices (you can ask your fishmonger to 'shuck' them if you are a little nervous of doing this yourself). Pass the juices through a very fine sieve into a small pan. Clean the shells thoroughly and warm them in a low oven.

2. Poach the oysters in their juices in the pan for no more than 45 seconds altogether, turning them over halfway through. Remove from the heat.

3. Bring the velouté to the boil and reduce a little, then season with a pinch of salt and a squeeze of lemon. Froth it up with a hand mixer or balloon whisk.

4. Melt the butter in another saucepan and add the eggs. Lightly scramble them and season with a little salt and pepper. Remove from the heat and mix in the cream to stop the eggs from cooking any further.

5. Fill the warm oyster shells with scrambled eggs and place the oysters on top. Cover with the velouté sauce and garnish with the caviar and chervil.

Tip > If you buy your oysters already shucked, they must be stored packed on a bed of ice in the fridge, and used within hours of purchase.

Ravioli of Langoustines with Truffles, Foie Gras Sauce

Raviolis de langoustines au truffe, sauce foie gras

Prepare the ravioli and the sauce, and shred and blanch the cabbage well in advance so all you have to do before eating is poach the ravioli, warm the sauce and briefly cook the cabbage. This dish looks very pretty on a simple white, deep-bottomed plate.

1 quantity Fresh Pasta (page 178)
20 langoustines, No. 1 or 2
10 g black truffle, very finely chopped
1 egg yolk
salt and freshly ground white pepper

Garnish
double quantity Sauce Albuféra
(page 158)
Buttered Cabbage (page 170)

1. Roll out the pasta to 1 mm thick. Cut into twenty 10 cm squares. Place on plastic film on a plate, cover with more plastic film and put into the fridge to rest.

2. Blanch the langoustines in boiling water for about 2 minutes, then drain. When cooled remove the heads, claws and shells. Dry the tails well and season with a little salt and pepper.

3. Remove the plastic film from the pasta and place the squares on a lightly floured work surface. Place a langoustine tail in the centre of each and sprinkle with a little fresh truffle.

4. Lightly beat the egg yolk, then brush over the edges of the pasta squares. Fold the pasta around the langoustines, insuring no air is trapped and that the edges of each of the ravioli stick firmly together. Trim with scissors, following the natural half-moon shape of the langoustine.

5. Fill a large pot with salted water and bring to the boil. When boiling rapidly add the ravioli and poach for 4 minutes. Drain well.

6. Whilst cooking the ravioli, warm the Albuféra sauce and cook the cabbage (this is best done at the last possible moment to maintain its colour).

7. Place five ravioli on each warmed plate and coat with the sauce. Garnish with a small mound of cabbage to the side.

Tip > Keep the langoustine heads, claws and shells, and freeze to make stocks and sauces.

Terrine of Foie Gras with a Sauternes Jelly

Terrine de foie gras en gelée de Sauternes

This will make enough for about eight portions. You could halve the quantities for four, but the terrine keeps well in the fridge and I promise you that any leftovers won't be left over for long. Start this two days before you need it.

4 x 800 g lobes of foie gras, softened (see Tip right)
$^1/_4$ bottle white port
$^1/_4$ bottle Armagnac
salt and freshly ground white pepper

Garnish
Sauternes jelly (see Madeira Jelly, page 145)
toasted slices of brioche

1. Pre-heat the oven to 150°C.

2. Take the foie gras out of the bags and split each lobe open. Turn a rounded bowl upside down and cover it with a clean damp cloth. One at a time, place each lobe of foie gras on the base of the bowl so that it opens up, with each half falling on either side of the bowl. With a very sharp paring knife, extract all visible veins, taking great care not to damage or cut into the lobe of foie gras too much.

3. Place the lobes in a dry, flat roasting tin and sprinkle lightly with salt (25 g of salt to each 1 kg of foie gras) and then with a little pepper. Pour over the port and Armagnac.

4. Place in the oven to heat for 5–10 minutes until the foie gras is soft and at blood temperature. Much of fat will run out and the lobes will shrink a little.

5. Very carefully remove them from the tin using a fish slice and place on a few layers of kitchen paper to drain. Very gently pat dry.

6. Use a terrine mould 20 cm in length and line it well with five layers of plastic film that overhang enough on all sides to fold up and cover the top. Place the pieces of foie gras in layers in the terrine mould. Do not press down; they will find their own level. Cover the top with the overhanging plastic film and chill in the fridge for 24 hours. The terrine will become firm.

7. Take the terrine out of the fridge just before serving and remove from the mould using the plastic film to ease it out. Remove the film, then cut the terrine into 1 cm slices.

8. Place a slice in the middle of each chilled plate and pipe Sauternes jelly around the edges. Serve with brioche toast.

Tip > The lobes of foie gras come in *sous-vide* bags. The foie gras will be hard from being chilled, so before use leave it out overnight at room temperature, still in its bag, to soften.

Sea Scallops Baked in Pastry with Lemon and Cinnamon

St Jacques à la croque

This dish never fails to please. The scallops are baked in their shells, tightly sealed with a pastry strip, which means that every bit of flavour is retained. The juices from the scallops form a stock that needs only a little butter to thicken it into a wonderfully light sauce. I only ever use diver-caught scallops as the farmed ones tend to be damaged and of inferior quality. Keep the scallop 'skirts' and trimmings for making the scallop stock.

8 large scallops

a little white wine vinegar

2 celery sticks

2 carrots

2 shallots, finely chopped

80 g unsalted butter

a tiny piece of cinnamon stick, crushed

a little grated lemon zest

300 ml Scallop Stock (page 144)

80 g Puff Pastry (page 179)

2 eggs, beaten

salt and freshly ground black pepper

1. Pre-heat the oven to 240°C.

2. Shell the scallops and clean them. Pat dry and place in the fridge to chill and 'set'.

3. Take four of the shells, both top and bottom, and clean thoroughly. Boil for 3 minutes in water with a little vinegar added to sterilize. Remove, dry and put to one side until cold to the touch.

4. Cut the celery and carrots into long julienne strips. Gently sweat the celery and carrot julienne and the shallots in 2 teaspoons of the butter for a few minutes until softened, then season with salt and pepper. Drain off any excess liquid.

5. Place the vegetable julienne in the bottom half of the sterilized scallop shells. Cut the scallops in half and place on top. Sprinkle very lightly with the crushed cinnamon and lemon zest. Gently spoon over the scallop stock and place the top shells in place.

6. Roll out the pastry into a thin strip, long and wide enough to seal the join on the scallop shells (about 30 cm x 4 cm). Egg wash the sides of shell at the join and attach the pastry, pressing with your fingers to seal. Bake the scallops for 10–12 minutes until the pastry seal is golden brown.

7. Remove from the oven, crack open the seal with a sharp knife and remove the top shell. Very carefully pour the stock from each scallop into a small pan and bring to a gentle boil, then whisk in the remaining butter. Pour this sauce back into the shells over the scallops and serve.

Vinaigrette of Leeks and Langoustines with Caviar
Vinaigrette de poireaux aux langoustines et caviar

Vinaigrette of leeks is a classic French bistro dish. It was Michele Tramer who thought of putting it into a terrine with langoustines and truffles (I've 'deconstructed' the dish for the photo). A very attractive terrine, it is easy to serve for a dinner party as all the work is done well ahead. The quantities given here make a terrine large enough for eight people as a starter. Any left over will keep well in the fridge.

8 langoustines, No. 2
30 medium leeks, trimmed
15 baby courgettes, trimmed
15 baby carrots, peeled
15 green beans, topped and tailed
1 large fennel bulb, leaves separated
salt and freshly ground white pepper

Garnish
green beans, split lengthways and
   blanched (optional)
Water Vinaigrette (page 149)
1 tsp caviar per person (optional)

1. Cook the langoustines in boiling water for 1–2 minutes, then drain. Remove the heads, claws and shells. Leave to cool.

2. Cook the leeks in boiling salted water until very tender. Drain thoroughly in a colander and leave to cool. Cook all the remaining vegetables separately in salted water until just tender – keep testing with the point of a knife; they should be al dente. Drain very well and leave to cool.

3. Use a terrine mould 20 cm in length and line it well with five layers of plastic film that overhang enough on all sides to fold up and cover the top. Place a layer of leeks on the bottom of the mould and on these place two lines of langoustine tails. Fill in the gaps lengthways with a layer of courgettes, then place another layer of leeks over these. Continue layering the langoustines and leeks with the carrots, fennel and green beans, until all the ingredients have been used.

4. Fold over the overhanging plastic film to cover the top and make two 2.5 cm slits in the film (this will allow air to be expelled, thus preventing bubbles). Place a heavy weight on top of the contents of the mould and leave in a cool place, or the bottom shelf of the fridge, for at least 24 hours.

5. Remove the terrine from the mould, using the plastic film to ease it out. Cut into slices and place one slice in the middle of each plate. Garnish with half moons of split green beans scattered around the edges, sprinkle with a little vinaigrette and top each slice with a dollop of caviar.

Old-fashioned Stuffed Savoy Cabbage with a Tomato Sauce

Chou farci à l'ancienne, sauce tomate

This dish can be eaten either as a starter, or a light main course with the addition of a salad and bread. It is simple peasant cooking, packed with great textures and loads of flavour. As with everything in cooking, you get out what you put in, so be sure your cabbage is crisp and fresh.

2 Savoy cabbages

Tomato Sauce (page 155), warmed for serving

salt and freshly ground white pepper

Stuffing

150 g pork fat, finely chopped

150 g lean pork, finely chopped

25 g chicken livers, trimmed

$^1/_2$ garlic clove, crushed

$^1/_2$ tbsp chopped parsley

10 g fine breadcrumbs

25 ml white wine

$^1/_2$ tsp brandy

$^1/_2$ egg

Braising liquor

1 carrot, peeled and diced

1 onion, diced

1 celery stick, diced

2 garlic cloves, chopped

1 bay leaf

sprig of thyme

2 tbsp olive oil

100 ml white wine

500 ml Veal Stock (page 140)

1. To make the stuffing, combine the pork fat, pork and chicken livers and mince finely, either by hand or with a food processor. Mix in the remainder of the stuffing ingredients.

2. Take 12 leaves from the outside of the cabbages and remove the main vein. Using 10 cm, 7.5 cm and 5 cm circular cutters, cut out four pieces of leaf in each of the three sizes.

3. Spread each leaf disc evenly with the stuffing. Place a 10 cm disc on a square of doubled plastic film. Lay a 7.5 cm disc over this and top with a 5 cm disc. Gather the corners of the film and twist the ends so that a ball of cabbage is formed. Make four balls in all.

4. For the braising liquor, sauté all the vegetables with the garlic and herbs in the oil in a medium saucepan until browned. Add the wine, turn up the heat and boil to reduce the liquid by half. Add the stock and bring back to the boil, then remove from the heat. Strain through a fine sieve and discard the vegetables.

5. Pour the strained liquor back into the pan and add the cabbage balls. Braise gently for 1 hour and 20 minutes.

6. To serve, remove each cabbage ball from the liquor using a slotted spoon, unwrap and place in the centre of a warmed deep-bottomed plate. Carefully pour the tomato sauce around it.

Tip > When buying a Savoy cabbage go for the heaviest ones you can find as a weighty cabbage is a good indication of tightly packed leaves and freshness.

Escalope of Foie Gras and Duck Egg on Toast

Escalope de foie gras chaude avec oeuf de canard en brioche

This is very posh egg on toast. Duck eggs have a richness of flavour that is not found in hen's eggs. The foie gras is cooked into the egg white and the yolk acts as a sauce to bring the whole thing together. A truly fabulous dish, either as a starter or a light lunch or late supper.

4 x 50 g escalopes of foie gras

75 g unsalted butter

4 duck eggs

4 individual brioches

salt and freshly ground white pepper

1. Cook the foie gras escalopes in a large non-stick pan until lightly caramelized on both sides. Remove from the pan and keep warm.

2. Melt the butter gently in the pan (if it will not take all the eggs, you will have to cook them two at a time), taking care not to burn it. Crack the eggs into the pan. Place a foie gras escalope into the white of each egg and cook gently until the white is perfectly set.

3. Whilst the eggs are cooking, halve the brioches and toast them.

4. Top the brioches with the duck egg/foie gras and season, then serve immediately.

Tip > When caramelizing the foie gras in stage one, make sure you don't cook it through as it will continue cooking within the white of the duck egg.

Parfait of Foie Gras with Madeira Jelly
Parfait de foie gras en gelée

This wonderfully luxurious pâté needs to be made at least 24 hours in advance, to allow it to set properly. For a less expensive version you can leave out the foie gras and make it entirely with chicken livers. It will still taste fantastic and have the same silky feel, but will be a little less rich and have slightly less flavour. The Madeira jelly is a brilliant accompaniment. The quantities here make a parfait that will serve eight generously.

100 ml ruby port

100 ml Madeira

50 ml brandy

150 g shallots, finely sliced

$1^1/_2$ garlic cloves, finely sliced

2 large sprigs of thyme

200 g fresh foie gras

200 g fresh chicken livers

2 tsp pink sea salt (*sel rose*), optional

1 tbsp white sea salt (*fleur de sel*)

4 eggs, at room temperature

400 g unsalted butter, melted and just above blood heat

Garnish

150 g unsalted butter

Madeira Jelly (page 145)

1. Pre-heat the oven to 160°C. You will need a terrine or pâté mould that is 30 cm x 11 cm and 10 cm deep.

2. Place the port, Madeira and brandy in a pan with the shallots, garlic and thyme. Boil rapidly to reduce until the liquid has almost all evaporated. Remove from the heat and discard the thyme.

3. Slice the foie gras and roughly chop the chicken livers. Place in another pan and sprinkle with the pink and white sea salt. Warm gently to just above blood heat.

4. Combine the port mixture with the foie gras and livers in a liquidizer and blend until completely smooth. You may need to do this in batches.

5. Add the eggs and blend well, then mix in the warm melted butter. Working quickly, push the mixture through a chinois sieve into a warmed container. Transfer to the terrine mould, using a spatula where necessary, and cover tightly with foil.

6. Place in a bain marie (a roasting tin half filled with boiling water is perfect for this) and cook in the oven for 1 hour and 10 minutes, checking occasionally to make sure there is still plenty of water in your bain marie.

7. Remove from the oven and bain marie and chill in the fridge for 24 hours.

8. To finish, melt one-quarter of the butter and soften the remainder. Emulsify the butter by whisking to lighten. Spread a thin layer on top of the parfait, then chill again so that the butter sets. Run a hot knife around the edges of the parfait and turn it out on to a board. Butter the other sides in the same way, chilling to set.

9. Meanwhile, pour a little still liquid Madeira jelly on to each serving plate and allow to set.

10. To serve, slice the parfait with a hot knife and place a slice just below the centre of each plate on top of the set jelly. Sprinkle with a little sea salt and coarsely ground white pepper. Serve with slices of good crusty bread.

Tip > *Sel rose* helps retain the colour of the livers.

Native Oysters with Citrus Fruits and Coriander

Huîtres aux citrus à la coriandre

This is a lovely way to eat oysters and looks very pretty on the plate. The citrus and coriander complement the wonderful 'essence of sea' tang that oysters impart, without overpowering it.

24 Native oysters, No. 2
2 Seville oranges
100 ml very good quality extra virgin olive oil
2 lemons
sprigs of young coriander

1. Open the oysters, taking care to retain as much of their juices as possible. Leave them on their half shells.

2. Carefully peel and segment the oranges, working over a bowl to catch all the juice. You want to have 24 orange segments totally devoid of any pith. If they are large oranges you will need to cut each segment in half. Set aside.

3. Squeeze the juice from the rest of the oranges into the bowl. Pour the juice into a small saucepan and boil gently to reduce to a thin syrup. Pour into a clean bowl and cover with the olive oil.

4. Carefully peel and segment the lemons. The segments of orange and lemon should be the same size.

5. To serve, carefully place a segment of orange and a segment of lemon over each oyster and add $\frac{1}{2}$ teaspoon of the orange juice dressing. Top each one with a sprig of coriander.

Tip > I serve the oysters on a bed of crushed rock salt, which sets them off beautifully, but this is entirely optional.

White Asparagus with Truffle
Asperges blanches au vinaigrette de truffe

The perfect starter for a summer's day. White asparagus is something of a delicacy and can be
a little more expensive than the more widely used green asparagus. If white is unavailable feel free
to use green, especially the wonderfully crisp English asparagus available from April onwards, which
is both plentiful and cheap.

24 medium, white asparagus spears
lemon juice
salt
sprigs of chervil

Dressing
50 ml sherry vinegar
100 ml truffle juice
100 ml olive oil
250 ml double cream
1 small whole truffle, roughly chopped

1. Remove the tough bottoms of the asparagus spears. Cook in boiling salted water, with a squeeze
   of lemon juice added, for 4–6 minutes until just tender but still slightly crisp.

2. To make the dressing, whisk together all the ingredients.

3. Drain the asparagus and place six spears on each warmed plate. Pour the dressing over the
   asparagus and garnish with fresh chervil.

Tip > Asparagus spears bend and snap naturally at the point at the bottom of the spear where
they become woody and inedible.

Terrine of Bresse Chicken, Sweetbreads and Foie Gras in Aspic
Terrine de volaille au ris de veau en gelée, sauce gribiche

This is everything that a terrine should be, and when served in the proper fashion atop a puddle of sauce gribiche it is a joy to eat. The tarragon and chervil lend a freshness to the plate and to the palate. This makes enough for 15 portions.

enough thinly sliced Parma ham to line the mould

700 g chicken fillets, cut into strips

olive oil

500 g fresh foie gras, sliced

800 g calves' sweetbreads, trimmed

200 g baby onions, peeled

100 g trompettes des morts (horn of plenty)

150 g girolles

500 ml Chicken Stock (page 138)

4 gelatine leaves, softened in cold water and squeezed dry

50 ml sherry vinegar

salt and freshly ground black pepper

Garnish

triple quantity Sauce Gribiche (page 153)

40 tarragon leaves

sprigs of chervil

1. Pre-heat the oven to 90°C, or the very lowest it will go. Line a terrine mould that is 30 cm x 8 cm in length and 8 cm deep with three layers of cling film. Arrange slices of Parma ham inside the mould, overlapping slightly, to line it evenly.

2. Sauté the chicken fillets in a little olive oil to seal. Drain well. Sauté the foie gras for a few minutes. Set aside.

3. Wrap the sweetbreads in cling film and cook in boiling water until firm. Refresh in iced water, then remove the film. Blanch and refresh the baby onions.

4. Layer all the prepared ingredients, along with the trompettes and girolles mushrooms, in the terrine mould to achieve a mosaic effect, making sure that each layer is well seasoned. Pour in the chicken stock.

5. Place the terrine mould in a bain marie (a roasting tin of water is fine), cover the top of the mould with foil and cook in the oven for 1 hour and 25 minutes.

6. When cooked, strain off the stock from the terrine mould into a bowl. Add the gelatine and sherry vinegar to the stock and pour back into the mould. Cool, then refrigerate to set.

7. To serve, turn the terrine out of the mould and slice carefully. Pour a little sauce gribiche on to each serving plate and place a slice of terrine on top. Garnish with a criss-cross of tarragon leaves and chervil.

....

Tip > Make the stock in advance and assemble the terrine on the day before it's needed to give it time to set properly.

Fifteen seconds is a lifetime when cooking fish. Perfection only lasts 15 seconds.

Chapter Three
Fish

Grilled Lobster with Garlic and Herb Butter

Homard grillé aux herbes

Nothing speaks of luxury and indulgence quite like lobster. The best lobsters in the world come from the icy cold waters of Scotland. This dish should be served with a simply dressed mixed salad.

4 x 600 g live lobsters

salt and freshly ground white pepper

few sprigs of flatleaf parsley or chervil

Garlic and herb butter

200 g unsalted butter, softened

30 g parsley, finely chopped

15 g shallots, chopped

10 g garlic cloves, finely chopped

2 tbsp Pernod

Stock

1 carrot, peeled and chopped

1 onion, chopped

1 celery stick, chopped

1 bay leaf

sprig of thyme

small handful of parsley stalks

20 white peppercorns

500 ml white wine

500 ml white wine vinegar

sea salt

1. First make the garlic and herb butter. Beat together all the ingredients with a couple of pinches of salt and pepper. Roll the mixture on plastic film into a log about 4 cm in diameter. Wrap in the film and chill in the fridge for about 30 minutes until it is set firm enough to slice.

2. Put the stock ingredients into a large pot with 10 litres water and simmer until all the vegetables are cooked. Remove from the heat and leave to stand for 1 hour. Strain the stock through a fine sieve into a clean pot and season with salt to taste.

3. Using a cooking thermometer to check, heat the stock to 80°C. Carefully take the bands off the lobsters' claws, then plunge the lobsters into the stock to cook for $3^1/_2$ minutes. Remove from the pan, wrap individually in plastic film and set aside in a warm place for 4–5 minutes, to relax and re-balance their juices.

4. Remove the claws from the lobsters, crack them open and carefully remove the meat in whole pieces. Do the same with the knuckles of the lobsters. With a large, sharp chopping knife, cut the body (or tail) of each lobster in half lengthways, from the head through to the end of the tail, taking care to preserve the shells. Remove the meat. Discard the brain sac, which is in the front of the head. Wash and clean out the lobster shells.

5. Pre-heat the oven to 200°C. Heat a baking dish large enough to hold all the lobster shells.

6. Place the garlic butter in a piping bag and pipe a small amount inside the shells from end to end. Cut each length of body/tail meat into three or four pieces and place them in the shell halves so that the red edge is visible. Put the knuckle and claw meat into the head cavity. Lightly cover all the lobster meat with garlic butter.

7. Place the lobsters in the heated baking dish and warm in the oven for 2–3 minutes. Don't let the butter burn.

8. Arrange on plates and garnish with parsley or chervil.

Shortcut > You could, if you so chose, buy your lobster already cooked, but nothing beats the flavour and texture of one that you have cooked yourself at home.

Poached Fillet of Turbot with Mussels and Clams Provençal
Turbot poché à la rochelaise, sauce bouillabaisse

A magnificent dish, this evokes all that is wondrous within the sea and the miracle of its glorious bounty. Turbot is to my mind the king of all fish, and when paired with the delicate flavour of mussels and clams is showcased to perfection. The bouillabaisse sauce is not so much a sauce as a soup – indeed it is the red mullet soup found on page 18, enriched with rouille. It complements the turbot perfectly and lends the dish a certain earthiness.

60 g unsalted butter

4 shallots, finely chopped

250 ml Fish Stock (page 139)

4 tbsp dry white wine

4 x 175 g pieces of turbot fillet

salt and freshly ground white pepper

Bouillabaisse sauce

400 ml Soup of Red Mullet with Saffron (page 18)

8 tbsp Rouille (page 150)

Garnish

20 new potatoes

olive oil

200 g each fresh mussels and clams

double quantity Tomato Fondue (page 163)

1. Pre-heat the oven to 220°C.

2. Boil the potatoes in salted water until just tender but still firm. Drain them, then slice widthways about 3–5 mm thick. Drizzle the slices of potato with a little olive oil and place on a very hot ridged grill pan or in a heavy-based frying pan. Cook for a second, then turn over on to the other side. Turn back again so that the slices have brown criss-cross markings on both sides. (If not using a grill pan they should be nicely golden brown on both sides.) Keep warm.

3. Cook the mussels and clams separately in a little water in a covered pan for a minute or so, just until they open. Remove from their shells.

4. Melt the butter in an ovenproof pan that is big enough to take all of the fish in a single layer. Sweat the shallots for 1–2 minutes to soften. Add the fish stock and wine, and season lightly. Bring to the boil, then place the fish in the pan. Cover with buttered paper and poach in the oven for 4–5 minutes.

5. While the fish is in the oven, heat the tomato fondue gently in a little olive oil. Add the mussels and clams, season and keep warm.

6. For the bouillabaisse sauce, bring the soup to a gentle simmer in a separate pan and whisk in the rouille. Keep warm.

7. To serve, arrange the mussels and clams in the middle of each plate. Lift the fish from its poaching liquor and place on top. Spoon the bouillabaisse sauce around the fish and place the potato slices in a semi-circle at the top of the plate.

Tip > Keep the liquor from the mussels and clams, and freeze it for future use when making seafood stocks and sauces.

Fillet of Red Mullet Niçoise
Filet de rouge à la niçoise

This dish has a rustic charm that is perfect for less formal entertaining. I would suggest making the ratatouille and the tapenade the day before and the sauce in the morning of the day it is required. The beignets need to be fried at the very last minute to insure they are puffed up and crisp. They are not essential, but do look lovely on the plate.

8 red mullet fillets of equal size, about 150 g each
25 ml olive oil
salt and freshly ground white pepper

Garnish
Tapenade Sauce (page 154)
Ratatouille (page 167)
Sage Beignets (page 173)

1. Carefully remove the pin bones from the mullet fillets, or ask your fishmonger to do this.

2. Bring the sauce to a gentle simmer and check the seasoning. Gently heat the ratatouille.

3. Season the red mullet fillets, then pan fry them in the olive oil over a gentle heat for about 2 $\frac{1}{2}$ minutes on the flesh side, without allowing them to colour. Turn them over and cook for a further 1 $\frac{1}{2}$ minutes on the skin side.

4. Meanwhile, shallow fry the sage beignets. Drain on kitchen paper.

5. Place the fish fillets on warmed plates, two on each. Pass the tapenade sauce through a small fine sieve directly on to the plate around the fish. Set a 5–7 cm ring mould at the top of the plate and spoon in the ratatouille. Top each fillet with a hot beignet and serve immediately.

Tip > I like to buy my red mullet on the smaller side rather than too big, as I find the flavour of the smaller fish is more delicate.

Confit of Wild Salmon with Salt Crystals, Tian of Aubergine

Confit de saumon sauvage au gros sel, coulis de tomate

Confit is a beautiful way to cook as it enhances the natural flavour of the food whilst imparting a wonderful melting texture. Duck is probably the best known food to confit, although many foods can benefit from being cooked in this way. The aubergine tian is an inspired garnish, as the plate requires a splash of colour and the sweet acidity that comes from marrying aubergine and tomato.

goose fat

4 x 250 g escalopes of wild salmon, pin bones removed

salt and freshly ground white pepper

Garnish

Aubergine Tians (page 172)

200 ml puréed cherry tomatoes

4 tsp olive oil

4 tsp tomato ketchup

120 g unsalted butter

sea salt flakes (*fleur de sel*)

1. Choose a pan large enough to accommodate all of the fish compactly and warm enough goose fat in it to cover the fish. When the fat is medium hot, submerge the escalopes and poach for about 4 minutes.

2. Meanwhile, warm the aubergine tians very gently, wrapped in foil in a low oven.

3. Place the cherry tomato purée in a saucepan and gently warm. Add the olive oil and ketchup, then whisk in the butter. Season and keep warm.

4. Remove the salmon from the fat and drain well on kitchen paper.

5. To serve, place the salmon escalopes on hot plates and surround with the tomato sauce. Sprinkle the fish with a few flakes of sea salt and garnish the top of the plate with the aubergine tians.

Tip > The *fleur de sel* is important both aesthetically and for the slight crunch that it gives.

Grilled Sea Scallops and Calamari with Sauce Nero

Panaché de St Jacques et calamar grillé, sauce nero

Here is a brilliant seafood dish that is uncomplicated and almost effortless – perfect for the home cook looking to impress. The sauce, made with the ink from the calamari, provides a wonderful colour contrast to the whiteness of the scallops, and lends a subtle flavour to the finished dish that belies its theatrical black and white façade.

12 medium scallops, shelled and trimmed
olive oil
24 baby squid, cleaned
salt and freshly ground white pepper
Sauce Nero (page 162), warmed for serving

1. Slice each scallop horizontally in half and season with salt. Heat a little oil in a non-stick pan, carefully place the scallops in the pan and cook gently for about 1 minute on each side to a very light golden brown. Keep warm.

2. Heat a little olive oil in another non-stick pan and cook the baby squid for a minute or so until crisp, then season with a little salt.

3. To serve, arrange six scallop discs in a ring in the centre of each warmed plate and top each one with a baby squid. Dot the sauce around them and place a small puddle of sauce in the centre. (This looks very effective on a plain white dinner plate.)

Tip > When preparing scallops it is important to insure you don't overcook them. A quick flash on each side in a hot pan and they'll be soft, yielding and a pleasure to eat. If overcooked they quickly turn rubbery and are not very pleasant.

Escalope of Salmon with Tarragon

Escalope de saumon sauvage à l'estragon

The combination of salmon and tarragon is divine. Though quite straightforward to prepare, this dish is another classic example of how good-quality ingredients need nothing more than the lightest of touches to create something wonderful.

4 x 150 g escalopes of wild salmon
1 tbsp olive oil
salt and freshly ground pepper

Garnish
200 ml Velouté for Fish (page 159)
400 ml Court-Bouillon for Seafood (page 143)
large handful of tarragon leaves, finely snipped
60 g unsalted butter

1. Combine the velouté sauce and court-bouillon in a saucepan, bring to the boil and add the tarragon. Leave to infuse for 10 seconds, then add the butter and stir in until melted. Season to taste. Keep warm.

2. Season the salmon, then fry gently in the olive oil in a non-stick pan for 2 minutes on each side.

3. To serve, pour the sauce into the centre of each warm plate and place a salmon escalope on top.

Tip > Buy the best salmon you can afford. It has to be wild – farmed salmon has little or no flavour and in worst-case scenarios has the consistency of cotton wool. Escalopes from a good-sized wild salmon that has spent its life swimming free in icy waters is what you're looking for here.

Fillet of Sea Bass with Fennel

Filet de loup de mer au fenouil, sauce vierge au basilic

The secret of this dish is to have your garnishes ready before you even think to start cooking the fish, because just the briefest cooking is required before dressing the fish and serving. To overcook or overcomplicate the subtle flavour found in a good piece of sea bass would be a travesty, so the golden rule is: keep it simple. Needless to say the fish should be line-caught and not farmed.

4 tbsp olive oil
4 x 175 g wild sea bass fillets
salt and freshly ground white pepper

Garnish
Sauce Vierge (page 151)
Confit of Fennel (page 170)
4 tsp Tapenade (page 154)
few sprigs of herbs, such as chervil and chives

1. Have the sauce and confit warming through before you start cooking the fish.

2. Heat the oil in a pan large enough to take all the fillets in one layer. Quickly seal the seasoned sea bass on both sides, then cook for a further 3 minutes on each side.

3. Remove the fillets from the pan and pat off excess oil. Spread them with the tapenade on the skin side, then place in the centre of hot plates.

4. Spoon the sauce around the fish and scatter the plate with the fresh herbs. Garnish with pieces of confit fennel and olives.

Tip > Rather than buy your fillets ready prepared, choose whole fish and have your fishmonger gut, scale and fillet them for you. You will end up with far fresher fish than the kind that comes wrapped in plastic.

Fillet of Cod Viennoise with a Grain Mustard Sabayon

Gratiné de morue à la viennoise, sabayon à la grande moutarde

Serving fish with mustard is an unusual but quite delectable combination. The mustard 'lifts' the fish and the herb crust creates the perfect foil for the mushrooms. Make the stocks, fondue, duxelles and soft herb crust in advance as well as the velouté for the sabayon, so that all that is required of you before serving is to assemble and cook the fish and transform the velouté into a sabayon at the last possible moment.

4 x 150 g pieces of cod fillet

4 tsp Dijon mustard

4 tsp Tomato Fondue (page 163)

double quantity Mushroom Duxelles
  (page 165)

half quantity Soft Herb Crust (page 165)

400 ml white wine

400 ml Fish Stock (page 139)

olive oil

lemon juice

salt and freshly ground white pepper

Garnish

Sabayon of Grain Mustard (page 157)

1. Pre-heat the oven to 220°C.

2. Season the cod, then lightly spread the top of each portion with the Dijon mustard, then with the tomato fondue and finally with the mushroom duxelles. Top all of this with the soft herb crust.

3. Place the fish on buttered paper in a shallow flameproof dish. Add the white wine, fish stock and a splash of olive oil and season this cooking liquor with salt, pepper and a little lemon juice.

4. Bring to the boil on top of the stove, then place in the oven and cook for about 5 minutes.

5. Meanwhile, pre-heat the grill to high and make the sabayon.

6. Place the cod on warm plates and pour the sabayon around. Place under the hot grill to colour the crust and sauce a golden brown. This should take about 1 minute. Serve immediately.

Tip > It is imperative not to overcook the fish when poaching as it will continue to cook when you place it under the grill.

Fillet of Brill Boulangère
Filet de barbeu à la boulangère, sauce lie de vin

This dish is a little more complex than some of the other fish dishes in this book, but is well worth the extra effort. The garlic confit looks great on the plate. Cooking garlic in this way brings out its natural sugars and the end result is surprisingly sweet and creamy – a perfect complement to the delicate flavour of the fish. I would recommend serving this dish with a simple green vegetable for colour, perhaps spinach or Savoy cabbage, and also some crisp sauté potatoes (see page 168).

2 large potatoes, peeled and finely sliced

50 ml goose fat

1 large onion, finely sliced

4 x 150 g brill fillets

200 g *crépine* (see Tip right)

2 tbsp olive oil

25 g unsalted butter

200 ml Fish Stock (page 139)

salt and freshly ground white pepper

Garnish

Sauce Lie de Vin (page 161)

double quantity Confit of Garlic (page 171)

1. Pre-heat the oven to 180°C.

2. Rinse the slices of potato to remove some of the starch, then pat dry using kitchen paper. Place the goose fat in a pan and gently warm, then add the potatoes and poach for 10 minutes; do not allow them to colour. Add salt and pepper whilst they are cooking. Drain well, reserving the goose fat, and leave to cool.

3. Cook the onion in exactly the same way using the same goose fat. Drain, once again reserving the fat (for later use in another dish).

4. Season each brill fillet and place a layer of onion and then of potato on each one.

5. Wash the *crépine* well and squeeze out all the water. Spread it out on the work surface, making sure there are no holes or any marbling. Cut it into four equal pieces and wrap a piece around each fish fillet and its topping, rolling over twice.

6. Heat the olive oil in a non-stick pan. Put in the four pieces of fish, potato and onion side down, and add the butter. Colour to a nice golden brown, about $1\frac{1}{2}$ minutes.

7. Line a flameproof baking dish with a large sheet of buttered paper. Put in the fish with the potato and onion facing up and pour in the stock. Bring to the boil on the hob, then place in the oven to cook for 7–10 minutes.

8. Meanwhile, heat the sauce and finish with cream and butter. Pan fry the cloves of garlic in a dry pan to crisp them up.

9. To serve, place a piece of fish in the centre of each warmed plate, arrange garlic cloves on the sides and spoon the sauce around.

Tip > *Crépine* is pig's caul fat, often used to wrap flat sausages (which are called *crépinettes*) and other meats. It is available from any good butcher.

Tronchonette of Turbot with Citrus Fruits, Fresh Coriander Oil
Tronchonette de turbot à l'orange

A lovely light dish that is just perfect for a summer's evening. The combination of the fruit and fish may seem a little unusual, but tastes just fantastic – kind of sweet and sour with the sauce adding real depth of flavour.

4 x 150 g pieces of turbot fillet

flour for dusting

olive oil for frying

salt and freshly ground white pepper

Garnish

4 segments of pink grapefruit

8 segments of lemon

pared zest of 2 lemons, cut into julienne strips

50 g fresh root ginger, peeled and cut into julienne strips

120 ml Stock Syrup (page 185)

20 ml white wine vinegar

4 celery sticks, strings peeled and cut into julienne strips

knob of butter

Sauce

120 ml Court-bouillon for Seafood (page 143)

6 segments of grapefruit

50 ml olive oil

2 tbsp chopped coriander

25 g unsalted butter

1. Put the grapefruit and lemon segments to warm in a bowl above the stove.

2. Blanch the julienne of lemon zest and ginger together briefly in boiling water. Drain and refresh in cold water, then blanch and refresh again. This will retain colour and keep them crisp.

3. In a clean pan combine the zest and ginger julienne with just enough stock syrup to cover. Bring to the boil and poach the julienne for about 15 minutes. Then add just enough of the vinegar to give a balanced sweet and sour taste. Leave to infuse off the heat.

4. Cook the julienne of celery with the butter and just enough water to cover until slightly tender but not soft. Drain and keep warm.

5. For the sauce, put the court-bouillon in a small saucepan and bring to the boil. Whisk in the grapefruit segments until they dissolve (only tiny cells of juice will remain). Whisk in the olive oil and the chopped coriander. Keep warm. Just before serving, finish the sauce by adding the butter in small pieces, incorporating it by swirling it in.

6. Season the pieces of fish and flour them lightly, then fry in the hot olive oil in a large frying pan over a high heat until cooked and light golden brown on both sides.

7. To serve, make a bed of celery in the middle of each warmed plate and place a piece of fish on top. Garnish the fish with the warmed citrus segments and sprinkle a little drained lemon zest and ginger julienne along the length of each fillet. Spoon the sauce around the fish.

Ragout of Shellfish with Leeks and Truffle

Ragoût de crustacés au blanc de poireau et truffe

If the sea were to be harnessed and put in a bowl, it would taste like this. A wonderful dish, this is aromatic, aristocratic and utterly, utterly decadent. I would serve this just with some good crusty bread to mop up the juices.

8 scallops, shelled and trimmed

12 langoustines

50 ml Vegetable Stock (page 142)

4 tbsp leek cut into fine julienne strips

120 ml Velouté for Fish (page 159)

120 ml Court-Bouillon for Seafood
(page 143)

8 oysters, shelled and juices retained

4 tsp chopped chervil

lemon juice

salt and freshly ground white pepper

Garnish

36 thin slices of truffle

chopped chervil

1. Cut each scallop horizontally into six very thin slices.

2. Blanch the langoustines in a large pan of rapidly boiling water for 10 seconds only; drain. Leave to cool slightly, then remove the heads, claws and shells.

3. In a small pan bring the vegetable stock to the boil. Add the leek and poach until tender but still firm. Drain and keep warm.

4. Put the fish velouté, court-bouillon and oyster juices in a pan with the chopped chervil. Warm through for 15 seconds, then add the scallops, langoustines and oysters. Poach them for about 1 minute. Make sure the liquid does not quite boil during this time.

5. To serve, taste and season with salt, pepper and lemon juice, then pour the ragout into warmed bowls. Scatter the leek julienne over the top and garnish with the truffle slices and chervil.

Grilled Dover Sole Niçoise
Sole grillée à la niçoise

Grilled Dover sole is a classic in its own right, served simply with a squeeze of lemon and perhaps some boiled potatoes dressed with a little butter and parsley. This is a slightly more refined version, giving the fish a Mediterranean twist whilst still allowing its true flavour to shine through.

4 x 450 g Dover soles, skinned
  and left on the bone
olive oil for frying
sea salt and freshly ground white pepper

Garnish
1 tsp chopped shallots
$1/4$ tsp crushed garlic

5 tbsp extra virgin olive oil
8 medium vine-ripened tomatoes,
  cut into a dice
12 black olives
8 very large canned anchovies, drained
  and rinsed
1 lemon, halved
large handful of sprigs of coriander

1. Pan fry the fish in a little olive oil for 6–7 minutes, turning halfway through (you may have to do this in batches). Season, remove from the pan and keep warm.

2. Whilst the soles are cooking, gently cook the shallots and garlic in a saucepan in 1 tablespoon olive oil; do not allow to colour. Add the tomatoes and cook until all the water from the tomatoes evaporates. This should take about 2 minutes. Remove from the heat and keep warm.

3. Using a small, sharp knife slice a petal from each side of each olive. You should end up with 24 oval discs. Cut each anchovy into quarters on a slant.

4. To serve, place the fish on warmed plates. Spread the tomato dressing lengthways down the centre of each fish, following the spine and working from head to tail. Top the dressing with a criss-cross of anchovy pieces, again working from head to tail. Put a petal of black olive into the centre of each criss-cross. The garnish should resemble a lattice. (Alternatively, arrange the garnish as shown in the photograph.) Drizzle a little olive oil on the plate down each side of the fish, about a tablespoon per plate, and top this with a very light squeeze of lemon.

Panaché of Langoustines and Sea Scallops with Cucumber and Ginger

Blanquette de langoustines et St Jacques au gingembre et concombre

As with a lot of fish dishes the preparation of this dish is relatively straightforward – indeed, apart from the pasta, there is hardly any actual cooking involved. It's more an assemblage of flavours and textures, with the delicate flavour of cucumber and pungent ginger acting as perfect foils for the fish.

1 cucumber, peeled

24 large langoustines, No. 2

115 g Fresh Pasta (page 178)

1 egg yolk

8 large scallops, shelled and trimmed

120 ml Court-Bouillon for Seafood (page 143)

120 ml Velouté for Fish (page 159)

25 g fresh root ginger, peeled and cut into fine julienne strips

knob of butter

lemon juice

1 star anise

salt and freshly ground white pepper

Garnish

16 tiny sprigs of chervil

4 star anise

1. Remove the seeds from the cucumber and cut it into 40 tiny, long, thin barrel shapes.

2. Blanch the langoustines in a large pan of rapidly boiling water for 10 seconds only; drain. Leave to cool, then remove the heads, claws and shells, insuring you keep the langoustines whole.

3. For the ravioli, roll out the pasta dough and cut out four discs about 5 cm in diameter. Mix the egg yolk with a pinch of salt, and brush onto the pasta to glaze.

4. Season four of the langoustines. Place one in the centre of each pasta disc and fold over to form a crescent, following the natural shape of the langoustine. Seal by pinching the edges together (make sure they are well sealed and have no air pockets). Trim the edges to enhance the crescent shape, either using a pastry wheel or sharp knife. Just before serving cook the ravioli in a large pan of boiling salted water for $2^{1}/_{2}$ minutes.

5. Cut the scallops horizontally in half or, if they are super large, into thirds. Place them with the remaining langoustines in a large pan along with the court-bouillon, fish velouté and ginger. Slowly bring to a simmer and cook very gently for about 40 seconds. Immediately remove the shellfish from the liquid using a slotted spoon and keep warm.

6. Add the cucumber and the knob of butter to the poaching liquid. Season to taste with a little lemon juice, pepper and star anise. Poach gently until the cucumber is tender but still firm.

7. To serve, place a langoustine in the centre of each warmed soup plate and place a ravioli on top of it. Arrange the scallops and remaining langoustines alternately around this.

8. Remove the star anise from the poaching liquid, then taste and adjust the seasoning, if necessary. Ladle equal amounts of poaching liquid, with the ginger and cucumber, over the shellfish in the soup plates.

9. Garnish each serving with four sprigs of chervil and put a star anise on the top of each ravioli.

Tip > Langoustines are fished in copious amounts in the Scottish seas. The majority of the catch is exported to France and Italy, which is such a shame as it means they remain quite hard to find in the UK and are very expensive. Should you manage to find them in good fishmongers they are well worth the cost – a langoustine tastes rather like lobster although slightly sweeter. Langoustines used to be commonly known as scampi, but they bear no resemblance to anything that has ever been served 'in a basket'.

Escalope of Wild Salmon with Tomato Ketchup Vinaigrette

Escalope de saumon sauvage aux herbes, vinaigrette de tomate

Here's a new creation of mine that sounds a little wacky but taste fabulous. The fresh herbs give the salmon depth and flavour whilst the ketchup vinaigrette gives the whole dish a fabulous sweetness tempered by the vinegar and Tabasco. No one ever manages to guess what the 'mystery' ingredient is. I like to serve this with a few sauté potatoes and a green salad.

4 x 200 g escalopes of wild salmon
olive oil

Vinaigrette
80 g very finely chopped shallots
1 tbsp finely chopped chervil
1 tbsp finely chopped chives
1 tbsp finely chopped tarragon
$\frac{1}{2}$ tbsp Worcestershire sauce
100 g tomato ketchup
8 drops of Tabasco sauce
300 ml olive oil
50 ml white wine vinegar

Garnish
sprigs of chervil

1. Mix together all the ingredients for the vinaigrette and set aside to infuse.

2. Pan fry the salmon fillet in a little olive oil until they are cooked but still pink in the middle – a couple of minutes on each side depending on the thickness.

3. To serve, place the fillets in the centre of warmed plates, top with a generous amount of the vinaigrette and add a few sprigs of chervil.

Grilled Lobster with Sauce Vierge
Homard grillé, sauce vierge

Here's another great lobster dish. I cannot stress enough that the sweet and juicy meat of this crustacean benefits from the lightest of cooking, and a sauce that complements the flavour rather than drowns it. Sauce vierge goes beautifully with lobster.

4 x 600 g lobsters, preferably live
Sauce Vierge (page 151)
few sprigs of chervil

Stock
1 carrot, peeled and chopped
1 onion, chopped
1 celery stick, chopped

1 bay leaf
sprig of thyme
small handful of parsley stalks
20 white peppercorns
500 ml white wine
500 ml white wine vinegar
sea salt

1. If using live lobsters, put all the stock ingredients into a large pot with 10 litres water and simmer until all the vegetables are cooked. Remove from the heat and leave to stand for 1 hour. Strain the stock through a fine sieve into a clean pot and season with salt to taste.

2. Using a cooking thermometer to check, heat the stock to 80°C. Carefully take the bands off the lobsters' claws, then plunge the lobsters into the stock to cook for $3^1/_2$ minutes. Remove from the pan, wrap individually in plastic film and set aside in a warm place for 4–5 minutes, to relax and re-balance their juices.

3. Remove the claws from the lobsters, crack them open and carefully remove the meat in whole pieces. Do the same with the knuckles of the lobsters. With a large, sharp chopping knife, cut the body of each lobster in half lengthways, from the head through to the end of the tail, taking care to preserve the shells. Remove the meat. Discard the brain sac, which is in the front of the head. Wash and clean out the lobster shells.

4. Cut each length of body/tail meat into three or four pieces and place them in the opposite side of the shell so that the red edge is visible. Put the knuckle and claw meat into the head cavity. Lightly cover the lobster with the sauce vierge.

5. Arrange on plates and garnish with parsley or chervil.

We live in a world of refinement, not invention.

Chapter Four
Meat

Poached Fillet of Beef with Baby Vegetables

Filet de boeuf à la ficelle, sauce gribiche

This is a dish that showcases beautifully all the fantastic produce that seems to appear as if by magic in our greengrocers in the spring, after a seemingly endless winter of heavier (and after a while rather dull) root vegetables. It utilizes a wide range of baby vegetables, which are to my mind seasonal produce at its very best. Poach the vegetables using the lightest of touches as it is vital they retain their delicate flavour as well as a slight bite along with their glorious jewel-like colours.

750 ml Beef Stock (page 141)
4 x 300 g fillet steaks, each about
   4 cm thick
bunch of baby carrots, trimmed and peeled
900 g baby new potatoes
bunch of baby leeks, white parts only

250 g shelled fresh peas
100 g asparagus
25 g baby red chard

Garnish
Sauce Gribiche (page 153)

1. Bring the stock to the boil in a pan that will accommodate all the fillets of beef.

2. Meanwhile, heat a dry non-stick pan, put in the fillets of beef fat side down and cook briskly for about 5 minutes until brown on all sides. Transfer the beef to the stock and simmer gently for 8–10 minutes. Remove the beef fillets from the stock and set them aside in a warm place to rest while you prepare the vegetables.

3. Cook the vegetables in boiling salted water for 5–8 minutes until just tender: add the potatoes and carrots first, the leeks and peas after 3 minutes, the asparagus 2 minutes later and the chard for the last 30 seconds. Drain well.

4. Slice the beef and arrange with the vegetables in four bowls. Serve with the sauce.

Tip > Though the stock takes a little time and a small degree of effort it is worth it for the end result, and you can make a lot more than you need and freeze in ice trays for future use in sauces or as a simple consommé. If you really don't have the time, then bought beef consommé can be used, although it will lack the richness of home-made stock. You will need the same amount, having added the reduced Madeira for flavour.

Roast Saddle of Rabbit with Rosemary, Fricassee of Langoustine

Râble de laperau aux langoustines, jus blond au romarin

This dish is the last word in elegance, using a meat that is far too rarely eaten in most households in the UK. I have a weakness for game and love cooking it. I grew up hunting rabbits with my dad and it remains to this day one of my favourite meats. The trompette mushrooms (which are also called horn of plenty) add a wonderful earthiness to the dish and are the perfect foil for the delicate flavour of rabbit.

2 saddles of farmed rabbit

10 tbsp clarified butter

16 langoustines

Sauce

400 ml Chicken Stock (page 138)

50 g unsalted butter

2 tsp whipping cream, whipped

2 sprigs of rosemary

salt and freshly ground black pepper

Garnish

double quantity Etuvée of Chicory (page 176)

100 g trompettes des morts

2 tbsp clarified butter

1. Pre-heat the oven to 240°C.

2. Trim the saddles of rabbit, leaving them on the bone. Cut off the belly flaps and keep these to one side. In an ovenproof pan, fry the saddles in 4 tablespoons of clarified butter until nicely golden brown all over.

3. Lift them out of the pan and arrange the belly pieces on the bottom of the pan. Place the saddles on top. Roast in the oven for about 8 minutes. Remove from the oven and set aside to rest. Leave the oven on.

4. Meanwhile, blanch the langoustines in boiling water for 1 minute. Drain. When they are cool enough to handle, remove the heads, claws and shells. Set aside.

5. Cut the belly pieces into very thin julienne strips and fry in 2 tablespoons of the clarified butter in the pan until very crisp. Drain well on kitchen paper and keep warm.

6. Drain the fat from the pan and replace with the stock. Stir and boil to reduce by half. Whisk in the butter, then the cream. Add the rosemary to infuse. Check the seasoning, then keep warm.

7. Warm the chicory, and pan fry the trompettes in 2 tablespoons clarified butter. When cooked, cut them into very fine julienne strips.

8. Quickly roast the langoustines in the remaining 4 tablespoons clarified butter for $1\frac{1}{2}$ minutes; do not overcook or they will be tough. Remove from the oven and keep warm.

9. To serve, remove the fillets of rabbit from the bone and cut each one lengthways in half. Arrange a piece on either side of each warmed plate with the crisp belly strips over the top. Pour the strained sauce around the meat, then place four langoustines between the pieces of rabbit. Finally, sprinkle the chicory around the plate, over the langoustines and around the fillet pieces, and then do the same with the julienned trompettes.

Tip > Needless to say, the rabbit should be wild, not farmed. If you can't get wild rabbit, don't bother to make this dish, as farmed has little or no flavour.

Grilled Rump Steak with Red Wine, Shallots and Marrow
Rumsteak à la bordelaise

I find that rump steak generally has a lot more flavour than do the leaner cuts of beef. As usual, it is imperative to buy the best meat you can afford as it will repay you tenfold on the plate. The marrow from the bone of a well-bred animal is a delicacy in its own right and transforms this dish from wonderful to sublime. Start this recipe the day before.

4 x 175 g rump steaks, well hung

100 ml vegetable oil

25 g unsalted butter

24 pieces marrow bone, 5 mm thick

salt and coarsely crushed (*mignonette*) white pepper

Sauce

4 shallots, finely chopped

100 ml each red wine and port

Red Wine Sauce (page 156)

1. Marinate the shallots in a mixture of the wine and port for 24 hours. Then simmer the shallot mixture to reduce down until it has almost evaporated. Add to the sauce and heat through gently. Keep warm.

2. Pan fry the steaks in the hot oil for about 3 minutes on each side, depending on the thickness. Add the butter halfway through the cooking. When the steaks are cooked to your taste, remove from the pan and allow to rest for 5 minutes.

3. Meanwhile, cook the pieces of marrow bone in a pan of simmering salted water for about 2 minutes. Drain well and remove the marrow from the bones.

4. To serve, place a steak on each warmed plate and pour the sauce over and around it. Place the marrow pieces on top of the steaks and season with a little salt and *mignonette* pepper.

Old-fashioned Braised Beef in Red Wine

Daube de boeuf à l'ancienne, garnis à la bourguignonne

As with most things, you reap what you sow – and here the quality of wine needs to be tip top. If you use plonk you'll end up with a dish that is mediocre, no matter how good the quality of the meat is. The golden rule is that if you wouldn't drink it, then why on earth cook with it?

1 x 2.75 kg ox cheek

1 medium onion

1 large carrot

3 celery sticks

1 large leek

1 head of garlic, cloves separated and peeled

sprig of thyme

1 bay leaf

$1\frac{1}{2}$ bottles Georges Duboeuf Beaujolais

50 ml olive oil

Veal Stock (page 140) to cover

salt and freshly ground white pepper

Garnish

Garniture Bourguignonne (page 175)

Parsnip Purée (page 174)

1. Pre-heat the oven to 180°C.

2. Trim the ox cheek of all fat and cut each cheek into four pieces. Place in a large dish.

3. Peel or trim the vegetables and cut into a large dice. Add to the dish together with the garlic and herbs, and cover with the red wine. Cover with plastic film and leave to marinate in the fridge for 8–12 hours.

4. Drain the meat, reserving the wine and vegetables separately. Strain the wine through a sieve into a saucepan and boil rapidly to reduce by half.

5. Pat the meat and vegetables dry with kitchen paper. Season the meat and, using about half of the olive oil, brown the pieces all over in a very hot pan. Drain and place in a suitable ovenproof casserole with a lid. Colour and caramelize the vegetables in the remaining oil, then drain well and add them to the meat.

6. Pour in the reduced red wine, then add enough veal stock to cover the meat and vegetables. Bring to the boil on the hob, then cover and place in the oven to cook for 4 hours.

7. Remove from the oven and allow the meat to cool in the liquor. When completely cold, remove any fat that will have gathered on the surface.

8. Before serving, reheat gently in the oven at the same temperature. Heat the garniture and parsnip purée.

9. To serve, place an equal amount of meat on each plate with plenty of the red wine sauce, sprinkle over the garniture and add a mound of parsnip purée.

Tip > Start this dish the day before, to allow the meat time to marinate in the wine and herbs. In fact, make that two days before. This dish actually benefits from being cooked a day in advance and kept, covered, in the fridge overnight, to really allow the flavours to develop.

Roast Suckling Pig with Apples and Spring Vegetables

Cochon de lait rôti à la printanière, jus marjolaine

Nothing can beat the sweetness of meat from a suckling pig (a baby piglet). The tender flesh needs very little in the way of seasoning – just some pepper and sea salt, which not only adds flavour but also ensures that you end up with fantastically crisp crackling. Apple is of course the accepted – and frankly the finest – accompaniment to pork, and the delicate flavour and slight crunchiness of baby vegetables will cut through the richness of the meat beautifully. The quantities given here will serve eight generously.

1 x 6 kg suckling pig, head off

vegetable oil

salt and freshly ground white pepper

Garnish

32 each of baby carrots, baby leeks and small asparagus spears

24 baby fennel bulbs

32 baby new potatoes, peeled

100 g unsalted butter

50 g small marjoram leaves

Jus Rôti (page 147)

24 sprigs of chervil

Apple sauce

6 Granny Smith apples, peeled, cored and diced

50 g unsalted butter

juice of $\frac{1}{2}$ lemon

pinch of caster sugar

1. Ask your the butcher to bone the pig and roll it so that it looks like a whole loin with skin all the way round. Also ask him to tie the roll and then score the skin lightly.

2. Pre-heat the oven to 180°C.

3. Brush the joint with a little vegetable oil and sprinkle with salt. Place in a roasting tin and roast for $1\frac{1}{2}$ hours, turning every 15 minutes.

4. Meanwhile, blanch the carrots, leeks, asparagus and fennel, in separate pans of boiling salted water to retain the individual flavours, until al dente, then drain and refresh in iced water. Cook the potatoes in boiling water until tender; drain. Set all the vegetables aside.

5. To make the apple sauce, sweat the apple dice in the butter with the lemon juice and sugar until the apples have broken down into a purée. Keep warm.

6. When the meat is cooked, take it out of the oven and remove the crackling. Return the crackling to the oven, at a higher temperature, to crisp up. Allow the meat to rest, covered to keep warm.

7. To reheat the baby vegetables and potatoes, warm them gently in an emulsion made from melting the butter with a little water. Season with a little salt as required.

8. Put the marjoram into the jus rôti and warm gently.

9. To serve, cut the meat into 1 cm slices and place an equal number of slices on each warmed plate. Arrange the drained baby vegetables and potatoes neatly over the meat with some crackling on top. Pour the marjoram sauce over the meat and the vegetables and garnish with sprigs of chervil. Serve the warm apple sauce on the side.

Shortcut > Instead of jus rôti, you could make the marjoram sauce using the roasting juices from the tin with half a chicken stock cube and a little water.

Rump of Lamb with Provençal Vegetables

Filet d'agneau avec légumes provençales

Great Mediterranean flavours encompass all that is so special about Provence and its gutsy style of cooking. The vegetables, which act as a colourful garnish for the lamb, need only be roasted in a hot oven with a sprinkling of olive oil and sea salt, or grilled, until just tender. Don't be tempted to add rosemary to them as it will drown out the flavour of the lamb. The aubergine tian adds a wonderful richness to the whole dish.

4 rumps of lamb, about 250 g each
4 tbsp clarified butter
salt and freshly ground white pepper

Sauce
1.4 litres Lamb Stock (page 146)
40 black olives, stoned and finely diced
4 knobs unsalted butter

Garnish
various simple vegetables, such as
    roast potatoes (use goose fat for
    a richer flavour), roast yellow and
    red peppers and grilled slices of
    courgette
Aubergine Tians (page 172)
Confit of Garlic (page 171)

1. Pre-heat the oven to 230°C.

2. Take the rumps off the bone, one by one, and skin them. You will be left with four small roasting joints. Season well. Brown all over in the clarified butter on the hob, then roast in the oven for 8–10 minutes, turning halfway through. Remove from the oven and leave to rest somewhere warm for 10–15 minutes.

3. Warm the garnish vegetables and tians, and fry the garlic to crisp up.

4. Bring the lamb stock to the boil. Check the consistency, then add the olives. Cook for 1 minute. Taste for seasoning, then whisk in the butter to give a gloss and slightly enrich.

5. To serve, slice each joint of lamb into eight or nine pieces and fan out across one side of each warmed plate. Cover generously with the sauce and garnish decoratively with the vegetables, garlic confit and aubergine tian.

Tip > Cook all your vegetables and prepare the sauce in advance.

Braised Pig's Trotters 'Pierre Koffman'
Pieds de cochon morilles, essence de morilles

This is my absolute favourite dish. It was created by Charles Barriere at his restaurant in Tours, and taught to me by Pierre Koffman. It's definitely a labour of love and needs a precise hand, but the end result is simply stunning. Despite the humble origins of the primary ingredient – the trotter, which is possibly the least expensive cut from the pig – it is a dish fit for a king, being both stylish and pleasing to the eye. Don't be put off by the seemingly long list of ingredients. I promise you that this dish will pay you back a thousand times over. It will serve six people.

6 pig's trotters (from the back legs
   only as they are bigger)
olive oil
2 carrots, peeled and cubed
1 celery stick, cubed
1 onion, cubed
250 ml dry white wine
750 ml Veal Stock (page 140)
sprig of thyme
$1/2$ bay leaf
salt and freshly ground white pepper

Filling
40 g dried morels
650 g veal sweetbreads
$1/2$ onion, diced
Chicken Mousse (page 164)

Sauce
2 chicken legs
100 g mushrooms, sliced
100 g shallots, chopped
$1/2$ head of garlic, sliced across
   to halve each clove

sprig of thyme
$1/2$ bay leaf
$1^1/_2$ tbsp sherry vinegar
$1^1/_2$ tbsp Cognac
400 ml Madeira
600 ml Veal Stock (page 140)
200 ml Chicken Stock (page 138)
4 dried morels
lemon juice
few drops of cream
knob of butter

Garnish
72 fresh wild mushrooms
25 g butter
double quantity Roast Button Onions
   (page 177), optional
Basic Mashed Potato (page 168),
   warmed for serving

1. Soak the trotters in cold water for 24 hours, then drain and pat dry. Singe off any remaining hairs, particularly between the toes. Scrape off the singed stubble and any stray hairs with a sharp knife.

2. Slit the underside of each trotter lengthways, starting at the ankle end. Cut the main tendon and then start to work off the skin by cutting around it with a sharp knife, close the bone. (Remember that the skin is effectively going to form a sausage skin, so be careful not to tear it.) Pull the skin right down and cut through the knuckle joint at the first set of toes. Continue to pull the skin off to the last toe joint. Snap and twist off the bones and discard them.

3. Pre-heat the oven to 220°C.

4. Heat 1 tablespoon olive oil in a heavy casserole dish and fry the carrots, celery and onion over a moderate heat for about 2 minutes. Add the trotters, skin side down, and the wine and boil until the wine is reduced by about half.

5. Add the stock, thyme and bay leaf. Bring back to the boil, then cover and place in the oven to cook for about 3 hours. During that time, shake the casserole from time to time to prevent the trotters from sticking to the bottom of the pot. Remove the trotters from the cooking liquid and leave to cool. They should be a wonderful oak brown colour.

6. To make the filling, soak the morels in cold water for 10 minutes; drain and rinse. Repeat this process one more time.

7. Remove the sinew and membranes from the sweetbreads (save the trimmings for the sauce). Cut the sweetbreads into cubes and fry these in a little very hot olive oil in a large frying pan over a high heat until they are golden brown with a crunchy texture.

8. Add the soaked morels and the onion and cook for 1 minute only. (Remember this mixture is to be cooked again once it is used to stuff the trotters.) Season well with salt and white pepper. Drain the mixture thoroughly in a colander and leave to cool.

9. When the mixture is cool, stir in just enough chicken mousse to bind the ingredients together. Taste and adjust the seasoning again, if necessary.

10. To make the sauce, heat some olive oil in a large frying pan over a moderate heat and fry the chicken legs and sweetbread trimmings until they are golden brown but not cooked through.

11. Add the mushrooms, shallots, garlic, thyme and bay leaf and stir well to combine. Deglaze the pan with the sherry vinegar, allowing it to bubble to get rid of the acidity. Deglaze in the same way with the Cognac. Add the Madeira and reduce until it looks caramelized. Pour in the stocks and 150 ml water to cover the chicken legs and vegetables. Drop in the dried morels and simmer for 20 minutes.

13. Strain the sauce, then pass the sauce through a fine sieve or muslin cloth several times, reserving the morels for a garnish for the potato if you wish. Just before serving, reduce the sieved sauce just a little to give a coating consistency, like a thin cream. Add a few drops of lemon juice and one or two drops of cream, then add the butter and a little pepper. Taste the sauce whilst adding these ingredients, to get exactly the right flavour to suit you.

14. To finish the trotters, cut out six large squares of kitchen foil big enough to wrap and seal a stuffed trotter. Butter one side of each square of foil, then place a trotter on it, skin side down. Pick out the little pieces of fat on the inside of the skin.

15. Divide the stuffing equally among the trotters. There should be enough stuffing to give the trotters bulk to retain the original shape. Roll the foil tightly around each trotter, making a sausage shape, and twist the ends to seal them securely. Put the parcels in the fridge to set for about 15 minutes.

16. Poach the trotters in a large pan of boiling water for about 12 minutes.

17. Meanwhile, prepare the garnish. Cook the wild mushrooms in half the butter in a large frying pan over a high heat until they produce their liquid. Drain the mushrooms in a sieve, then cook again for minute or two in the remaining butter. Keep warm.

18. To serve, remove the trotters from the poaching water, unwrap them and carefully place one, intact skin up, on each warmed plate. If using, arrange the onions on each plate, in lines above and below the trotter. Scatter the wild mushrooms over the trotters. Place a pool of mashed potato, about the same width and length as the trotter, alongside it at the top of the plate and, if using, dot it with sliced morels reserved from the sauce. Coat the trotters with the sauce and spoon more sauce onto the plate.

Tip > You need to start cooking this at least a day in advance, to have enough time to soak your trotters adequately. I would suggest making the various stocks and sauces well ahead.

Breast of Pigeon with Foie Gras Wrapped in Cabbage

Pigeon au foie gras en chou, pommes mousseline

The flavour of these little birds is wonderfully rich. The trick to this dish is to retain as much of the pigeons' natural juices as possible whilst insuring the foie gras doesn't liquefy during the steaming process – hence the whole is wrapped first in a cabbage leaf and then in caul fat. I suggest you serve this with creamed potatoes.

4 Savoy cabbage leaves (taken from the outside)
4 breasts of squab pigeon from Bresse, wing bone attached,
    from birds 550–600 g in weight
4 x 50 g escalopes of foie gras
500 g *crépine* (pig's caul fat)
40 g clarified butter
salt crystals and coarsely crushed (*mignonette*) white pepper

1. Blanch the cabbage leaves in very hot water for about 1 minute, then drain and refresh in iced water. Pat dry. Using a very sharp knife shave the raised centre stalk on each cabbage leaf so that it is flush with the leaf itself.

2. Lay the pigeon breasts on a work surface and top each one with an escalope of foie gras. Wrap each breast in a cabbage leaf, then wrap in the *crépine* to seal.

3. Steam, either in a steamer or in a bamboo basket, over a pan of boiling water for 6 minutes in total – 3 minutes on each side. Leave to rest in a warm place for about 5 minutes.

4. Pan fry very gently in clarified butter without colouring. Remove from the heat and sprinkle with salt crystals and *mignonette* pepper. Serve immediately.

Tip > It is important that there are no tears in either the cabbage leaves or the pig's caul, to insure there will be no leakage.

Braised Oxtail in Crépinette
Queue de boeuf en crépinette

Just the thing for a winter's day, this dish makes a perfect Sunday lunch in place of the usual roast. The slow cooking really brings out the flavour of the meat and the *crépine* wrapping adds a wonderfully rich and unctuous quality. Admittedly it's a little labour-intensive but it's worth the effort – and once it's in the oven you can just forget about it for 3 hours.

2.25 kg oxtail, trimmed and jointed
750 ml red wine
vegetable oil
3 large carrots, peeled
2 large onions
3 celery sticks
1 head of garlic, cut horizontally in half
1 tsp brandy
30 g plain flour
2.5 litres Veal Stock (page 140)
sprig of thyme

1 bay leaf
1 small celeriac, peeled
200 g *crépine* (pig's caul fat)
salt and freshly ground white pepper

Sauce
500 ml red wine
150 ml port
25 g chilled unsalted butter, diced
1 tsp double cream

1. Trim any excess fat from the outside of the pieces of oxtail, then leave them to marinate in the red wine overnight.

2. Pre-heat the oven to 160°C.

3. Lift the oxtail out of the wine and pat dry. Strain the wine through a fine sieve into a pan and boil to reduce by three-quarters, skimming off any impurities.

4. Meanwhile, coat the bottom of a large, heavy-bottomed pan with vegetable oil and heat until almost smoking. Season the oxtail pieces, then sear them all over in the hot oil until they are a good, deep, dark colour. Remove and drain.

5. Cut two of the carrots, the onions and celery into large chunks. Gently fry these vegetables and the garlic in the same oil until they are golden brown. Add the brandy and cook until it has almost evaporated. Add the reduced red wine marinade and continue to reduce.

6. When almost a syrup, add the oxtail pieces and stir in. Sprinkle in the flour (you can brown it in a dry pan first for extra flavour, if you wish) and stir together. Continue to cook for 5 minutes.

7. Pour in 2 litres of the veal stock and bring to the boil, then turn down to a gentle simmer. Add the thyme and bay leaf, cover with a lid and place in the oven to cook for $2^1/_2$–3 hours until the meat is tender enough to fall easily off the bone.

8. Lift the oxtail from the cooking liquid, and remove and discard all the pieces of vegetable. Set aside.

9. Pass the cooking liquid through a fine sieve and then through a muslin cloth three or four times to remove any impurities or solids. Put one-third of the cooking liquid into a pan and reduce it on the stove until very thick. Remove from the heat and keep warm. The other two-thirds of the liquid will be used to make the sauce (see below).

10. Cut the celeriac and remaining carrot into a 1.5 cm dice. Cook these separately in a little hot vegetable oil until golden brown. Drain and cool.

11. Carefully take all the meat from the oxtail pieces, keeping it in fairly large pieces rather than smaller flakes. Leave behind as much fat and gristle as possible. Add the celeriac and carrot dice and the reduced third of the cooking liquid to the oxtail meat. Gently combine and allow to cool.

12. When cool, mould the mixture into four balls (a 120 ml ladle is good for this process). Wrap the balls individually in plastic film and allow to 'set' in the fridge.

13. Cut the caul fat into four pieces without holes or large veins of fat. Lay one piece flat on the work surface. Unwrap one oxtail ball from its plastic film and place on the caul fat. Roll the fat around the ball, fixing the ends of the fat together. Do the same with the remaining balls.

14. To make the sauce, reduce the red wine and port together to a syrup, then add the remaining two-thirds of the cooking liquid. Reduce this to a consistency that will coat the back of a spoon. Whisk the butter into the sauce to enrich it and give it a glossy shine, then add the cream. This helps to stabilize the sauce. Set aside.

15. When ready to finish the dish, pre-heat the oven to 220°C.

16. Place the oxtail balls in a small tin or casserole with the remaining veal stock – the stock should cover them by one-third – and put into the oven to heat for at least 10 minutes. Keep spooning the stock over them so that they become glazed.

17. Meanwhile, reheat the sauce and correct the seasoning. Serve an oxtail ball on a puddle of the sauce and spoon a little over the top as well.

Tip > This needs to be started a day or two in advance and I suggest you make the stock and sauce ahead of time. The caul fat must be well washed to be sure that all the blood is removed. The best way to do this is to leave it under cold running water for about 8 hours.

Pot Roast of Pig's Head with Honey and Cloves

Tête de cochon braisée au miel et clou de girofle

I don't suppose many of you will attempt this dish at home. The reason I have included it here is that it is a wonderful example of how peasant food – born of poverty, where every last scrap of the animal was eaten – has yielded delicacies such as this, which today are showcased as haute cuisine in celebrated restaurants by Michelin chefs.

1 pig's head

2 large onions

2–3 large carrots

2 tbsp olive oil

250 g liquid honey

1 litre Veal Stock (page 140)

1 litre Chicken Stock (page 138)

20 cloves

2 sprigs of fresh thyme

1 bay leaf

dash of white wine vinegar

1 shallot, finely chopped

1 tbsp clarified butter

15 g unsalted butter

salt and freshly ground white pepper

Garnish

75 g asparagus spears

75 g baby leeks

75 g baby carrots

sprigs of chervil

1. Ask your butcher to cut the pig's head in two and to remove the brain and tongue whole. Reserve the brain.

2. Put the head and tongue in a large pan of cold water and bring to the boil. Drain and refresh in cold water. Place in a flameproof casserole.

3. Pre-heat the oven to 150°C.

4. Brown the unpeeled onions and carrots in the olive oil in a large saucepan. Add the honey and stir to caramelize the vegetables. Add to the pig's head and tongue in the casserole, place on the hob and turn over to glaze. Season.

5. Cover with the veal and chicken stocks and add 16 of the cloves, a sprig of thyme and the bay leaf. Cover the casserole, place in the oven and cook for $3^{1}/_{2}$ hours until the jaw bone starts to loosen from the head.

6. Meanwhile, prepare the brain. Remove the membrane, put the brain in a pan and cover with water. Add the vinegar, shallot and remaining thyme and bring to the boil. Remove from the heat and leave to cool in the water.

7. When the pig's head is cooked, remove it from the pot and take the meat from the cheeks, temples and snout. Set the meat aside with the tongue and keep warm.

8. Strain the cooking juices through a muslin-lined sieve into a pan and reduce to a coating sauce. Add the remaining cloves and leave aside to infuse.

9. When ready to serve, lightly cook the garnish vegetables in boiling salted water; drain. Drain the brain well and pan fry in the clarified butter to a golden brown all over. Warm the sauce, remove the cloves and stir in the butter.

10. To serve, place a little of each of the different meats, including the tongue and brain, on warmed plates. Cover with the sauce and arrange the vegetables in the centre. Garnish with chervil.

Tip > If you want to try this but don't want to use the whole head, it can be made using pig's cheeks, which have a wonderful sweet flavour.

Tranche of Calf's Liver, Sauce Bercy
Escalope de foie de veau Bercy

Calf's liver is such a treat, especially when it is cooked to pink inside and served with the proper accompaniments such as here. The crisp bacon adds bite and the spinach great colour, whilst the potato perfectly complements the smooth texture of the liver.

4 thin slices of calf's liver, about 175 g each
plain flour
vegetable oil
salt and freshly ground pepper

Garnish
900 g baby spinach leaves
50 g unsalted butter
8 wafer-thin slices streaky bacon
4 large sage leaves
Pommes Purée (page 169)
Sauce Bercy (page 160)

1. Pre-heat the grill.

2. Cook the spinach with the butter and 50 ml water for a few minutes until only just wilted. Drain if necessary. Season with salt and pepper and keep warm.

3. Grill the bacon until crisp. Meanwhile, deep fry the sage leaves in hot vegetable oil for a few seconds until crisp. Drain the bacon and sage leaves well on kitchen paper and keep warm.

4. Season the liver slices with salt and pepper, and flour them lightly. Heat 50 ml vegetable oil in a large wide pan and fry the liver until golden brown on both sides and pink in the middle – 3–4 minutes in total.

5. To serve, place the spinach in the middle of the warmed plates and arrange the liver over the top. Put the crisp bacon on top of the liver along with the sage leaves. Add a *quenelle* (use two spoons for shaping this) of potato at one side of the spinach and liver on each plate.

Tip > Prepare the potato purée and sauce in advance and keep warm or reheat for serving.

Breast of Duck with Olives

Magret de canard aux olives, chou à la crème

A typical French bistrot dish, this is full of flavour and simple to prepare. The breasts should be from wild ducks if possible. I enjoy this dish served with pommes purée (see page 169).

4 x 200 g duck breasts

175 g puréed black olives (keep the stones)

25 ml goose fat

salt and freshly ground white pepper

Creamed cabbage

1 Savoy cabbage

1 large carrot, peeled

50 g peeled celeriac

50 ml goose fat

50 g smoked streaky bacon, cut into lardons

100 ml double cream

Garnish

Red Wine Sauce (page 156)

2 tbsp double cream

25 g chilled unsalted butter, diced

1. Pre-heat the oven to 220°C.

2. Chill the duck breasts well, then remove some of the excess fat with a sharp knife. Make a slight incision, cutting horizontally, to form a pocket between the fat and meat.

3. Place the puréed olives in a piping bag and lightly fill the pocket in each breast. Do not overfill or the purée will run out during cooking. Chill until ready to cook.

4. To prepare the cabbage, discard the outer leaves and the core, and cut the remainder into baton-sized strips. Cut the carrot and celeriac into thick julienne strips. Heat one-third of the goose fat in a good-sized, heavy-bottomed pan and sauté the lardons of bacon. When they start to colour, add the carrot and celeriac and cook for a few minutes. Drain in a colander.

5. Place the pan back on the heat, add half the remaining goose fat and cook the cabbage in it for a few minutes. Remove and add to the bacon, carrot and celeriac. Set aside.

6. Pan fry the duck breasts in the goose fat, searing them on both sides, then turn skin side down. Place in the oven to cook for 5 minutes. Remove and allow to rest for 5 minutes.

7. Meanwhile, put half the red wine sauce into a small pan, add the olive stones and gently reduce by half. Add the rest of the sauce, the cream and the butter. Strain the sauce and keep warm.

8. Reheat the cabbage mixture in the remaining goose fat and season to taste. Pour in the double cream and reduce lightly just to coat the vegetables.

9. To serve, place the cabbage at the top of each plate. Arrange the duck breasts, either whole or sliced thinly, below the cabbage and pour the sauce around.

Only ever pay
big money for food
when the chef is
behind the stove.

Chapter Five
Desserts

Vanilla Cream with Champagne-poached Strawberries

Crème de vanille aux fraises pochées au Champagne

In this classic pudding the main ingredient is double cream flavoured with vanilla, so it stands to reason that you should buy the best and freshest cream you can find. There are some specialist dairy farms around the UK that are producing wonderful creams and cheeses. The poached strawberries complement the creaminess perfectly and add a lovely burst of colour.

2 gelatine leaves

80 g caster sugar

500 ml double cream

3 vanilla pods, split lengthways

2 tbsp rum

sprigs of mint

Poached strawberries

$1/_4$ bottle Champagne

150 g caster sugar

1–1$^1/_2$ punnets strawberries, hulled

1. Place the gelatine leaves in cold water to soften.

2. Combine the sugar, cream and vanilla pods in a saucepan and heat to just below boiling point. Remove from the heat.

3. Squeeze the gelatine dry, then stir into the warm cream until completely melted. Add the rum. Pass through a fine sieve and divide among four 150 ml pudding moulds. Place in the fridge to set, which will take at least 4 hours.

4. Bring the Champagne and sugar to the boil, stirring to dissolve the sugar. Pour over the strawberries and leave to cool, then chill.

5. To serve, loosen the sides of the pudding from the moulds, then turn out on to four plates. Spoon the strawberries and juices around the creams and garnish with mint.

Tip > This is equally delicious made with fresh raspberries and raspberry coulis.

Soufflé of Raspberries
Soufflé des framboises

The Golden Rule when making a soufflé is never to open the oven door until the cooking time has elapsed, no matter how tempted you may be to have a peek. And then a soufflé needs to be served the moment it comes out of the oven.

25 g unsalted butter

16 whole raspberries

125 ml framboise (raspberry eau de vie)

500 ml fresh raspberry purée, sieved

15 g cornflour

320 g caster sugar

12 egg whites

icing sugar

1. Pre-heat the oven to 180°C. Thoroughly butter the inside of four soufflé dishes measuring 7.5 cm in diameter and 6.5 cm deep.

2. Marinate the whole raspberries in the framboise. Set aside until they are to be used.

3. Make a raspberry reduction by placing the sieved purée in a pan and reducing it by half. Mix the cornflour with 25 ml of the framboise marinade and add this to the reduced purée. Cook, stirring constantly, until thickened, then remove from the heat.

4. Dissolve 100 g of the caster sugar in 75 ml water and boil up to 120°C. Add to the raspberry mixture, mix well and leave to cool.

5. Place the egg whites in a bowl and whisk until they start to thicken and take shape. Slowly add the rest of caster sugar 50 g at a time, whisking constantly, until all the sugar is incorporated.

6. Put the cooled raspberry reduction in a bowl and whisk in one-third of the egg whites, then very carefully fold in the rest of the egg whites. Take care you don't over-mix, as the more you stir the more air you'll lose from the egg whites.

7. Half fill the soufflé dishes with the raspberry mixture, then place three drained marinated raspberries in the centre of each dish. Fill to the top with the rest of the raspberry mixture and scrape off any excess with a palette knife. Run your finger round the edge to push the mixture away from the sides. Cook in the oven for 10 minutes.

8. Set each soufflé dish on a plate, dust with a little icing sugar and top each with a marinated raspberry. Serve immediately.

Tip > This can also be made with blackberries, replacing the framboise with crème de cassis.

Iced Hazelnut Nougat with Raspberry Coulis

Biscuit glacé au noisette, coulis de framboise

A very unusual dessert, this is based on my childhood discovery of nougat in Italy, where it is prized almost more than chocolate and is indeed given in huge blocks to children at Easter in the place of chocolate eggs. Each region has its own version of 'torrone' (to use the Italian name), which varies from very soft and almost mousse-like to rock hard and stuffed full of various candied fruits and nuts. This is a frozen nougat, incredibly smooth with a surprising crunch. The beauty of this is that it can be prepared well in advance. It will serve at least eight portions.

425 g caster sugar

15 g shelled hazelnuts

6 egg whites

450 ml double cream

double quantity Raspberry Coulis (page 182)

40 fresh raspberries

8 sprigs of fresh mint

1. Line a terrine mould measuring 30 cm x 7.5 cm with greaseproof paper and put into the freezer at its coldest setting to chill.

2. To make the praline, heat 150 g of the sugar in a pan until it melts and begins to make a caramel. Stir in the hazelnuts. Pour the mixture on to a cold, oiled tray to set. When it is hard crush it into pieces.

3. Whisk the egg whites, then gradually whisk in the remaining sugar to make a stiff meringue. Separately whip the cream until it makes stiff peaks. Fold the whipped cream into the meringue and carefully mix in the crushed praline.

4. Fill the ice-cold terrine mould to the top with the praline mixture and return to the freezer to set hard.

5. To serve, remove the terrine from the freezer and the iced nougat from the terrine. Cut into 2.5 cm slices. Put a slice on each plate, surround with raspberry coulis and decorate each portion with five raspberries and a sprig of mint.

Pear Tart Tatin
Tarte Tatin de poire

Here is one of my oldest and most treasured recipes for this classic tart, which is a perennially popular pudding, everyone's favourite. Tart Tatin is best made in a copper pan. These quantities serve two; for four, double everything including the size of the pan.

100 g unsalted butter

90 g caster sugar

pinch of ground cinnamon

2 pears, peeled, cored and halved

1 cinnamon stick

100 g Puff Pastry (page 179)

1. Pre-heat the oven to 180°C.

2. Spread the butter on the bottom of a copper pan measuring 15 cm in diameter, and sprinkle the sugar and cinnamon over it evenly. Place the pear halves, rounded sides down, symmetrically in the pan. Place the cinnamon stick on the diagonal in the centre.

3. Roll out the puff pastry to a disc with a diameter of 18 cm. Trim the edge neatly, then lay the pastry over the pears and tuck down the sides between the pears and the pan.

4. Place the pan on the hob over a medium heat and cook, watching carefully, until the butter and sugar make a light brown caramel – you will see it bubbling up around the edges of the pan. This will take a few minutes.

5. Transfer the pan to the oven and bake for 30 minutes until the pastry is golden brown.

6. To serve, set the pan on a medium heat until the caramel starts to bubble again. Give the pan a shake, then turn out the tart, upside down, on to a serving plate. Serve with double cream.

Tip > I have made this tart both with apples and with pears – they work equally well. For the apple version I like to use English Cox's Orange Pippins, as they are good firm apples that don't collapse during the cooking process and have a great aromatic flavour.

Harvey's Lemon Tart
Tarte au citron

This is my most preferred pudding and a wonderful way to finish a meal. Any chef worthy of his name will have a lemon tart on his menu and this one has been with me since Harvey's, my first ever restaurant – we made it twice a day: in the morning just before lunch service and again in the early evening around 7pm just before dinner, so it was always fresh and aromatic. This tart will serve eight. I suggest you don't make it any smaller as it tends to disappear rather quickly. I generally allow my lemon tart to speak for itself, but you could add a little whipped cream or, as shown in the photograph, a small lemon soufflé to garnish.

Pastry

500 g plain flour

175 g icing sugar

250 g unsalted butter, at room temperature

grated zest of 1 lemon

1 vanilla pod, split open

$1\frac{1}{2}$ eggs, beaten

Lemon filling

9 eggs

400 g caster sugar

grated zest of 2 lemons

juice of 5 lemons

250 ml double cream

Decoration

50 g icing sugar

sprigs of mint

1. Sift the flour and icing sugar on to a work surface and work in the butter. Make a well in the centre and add the lemon zest and seeds scraped from the vanilla pod. Add the eggs. Knead the mixture with your fingers, working as quickly as you can, until everything is combined to a smooth dough. Wrap in plastic film and leave to rest in the fridge for at least 30 minutes.

2. Pre-heat the oven to 180°C.

3. Grease a flan tin with a removable base that is 20 cm in diameter and 3.75 cm deep. Roll out the pastry on a lightly floured surface to a disc large enough to line the tin and allowing an overhang of not less than 1 cm. Lay the pastry gently into the tin.

4. Line the pastry case with greaseproof paper and fill with enough dry baking beans or lentils (or indeed any dry pulses) to insure the sides as well as the bottom are weighted. Bake for 10 minutes. Remove the beans and greaseproof paper and trim off the overhanging pastry, then return the flan case to the oven to bake for a further 10 minutes.

5. Meanwhile, make the lemon filling. Whisk the eggs with the caster sugar and lemon zest in a large bowl until smooth. Stir in the lemon juice, then add the cream. Continue to whisk until all the ingredients are thoroughly combined. Skim any froth from the top.

6. Reduce the oven temperature 120°C. Pour the cold filling into the hot pastry case (this will insure that the case is sealed). Bake for 30 minutes. Remove from the oven and leave to cool and set for about an hour.

7. When ready to serve, preheat the grill to very hot. Sift the icing sugar over the top of the tart and place it under the grill to caramelize the sugar to a light golden brown. Alternatively, you can just sprinkle the tart with icing sugar without caramelizing it. Cut the tart into slices and decorate each with a sprig of mint.

Tip > The secret of a really good lemon tart is that the filling should be firm and clear and the pastry light and crisp. It should never be cut immediately after it is cooked as it needs time to cool and set for at least an hour, or the filling will be too runny.

Prune and Armagnac Ice Cream
Glace de pruneau et Armagnac

Unlike so many of the gadgets that seem to find their way into a home kitchen collecting dust (the somewhat uncalled-for electric bread maker springs to mind – there is nothing quite so satisfying as kneading and proving your own bread and you don't need a machine to do it), an ice cream maker is a very practical and enjoyable addition to any kitchen. The combination of prunes and Armagnac in this ice cream is delightful and well worth buying a good bottle of Armagnac for. And be sure to use Agen prunes – Agen in France produces the best prunes in the world.

200 g pitted Agen prunes
enough Armagnac to cover
250 ml Vanilla Ice Cream (page 183)
sprigs of mint

1. Soak the prunes in Armagnac for a few hours, then remove and chop finely. Reserve the Armagnac.

2. Mix 65 ml of the Armagnac with the softly churned vanilla ice cream, then continue churning in the ice cream maker until set.

3. To serve, place two scoops of ice cream on each plate and surround with the prunes and remaining Armagnac, then decorate with a sprig of fresh mint.

....

Tip > If you don't have an ice cream maker then you can use bought ice cream here. There are some really very good brands on the market now, although as usual home-made is always best.

Jelly of Red Fruits, Raspberry Coulis
Gelée de fruits rouges, sirop de framboise

This dessert is an alternative to that old favourite Summer Pudding, but is much lighter and cleaner. I love it because it conjures up memories of childhood in a way that no other pudding can – no child's birthday party would be complete without jelly and ice cream. This version is a lot more sophisticated but just as charming.

250 g caster sugar

325 ml red wine

2 star anise

4 gelatine leaves, soaked in cold water to soften

1 punnet each of raspberries, strawberries, blackberries and blueberries

Raspberry Coulis (page 182)

1. To make up the jelly, put the sugar and red wine into a saucepan with the star anise and dissolve the sugar over a gentle heat. Take off the heat. Squeeze out the softened gelatine, add to the mix and stir until completely melted. Leave to cool but not to set.

2. Arrange a layer of raspberries on the bottom of four dariole moulds. Pour over a little of the jelly and put into the fridge to set. Add a layer of sliced strawberries, just cover with jelly, and allow to set. Add a layer of blackberries and more jelly, then allow to set. Finally, add the blueberries and the rest of the jelly. Refrigerate for 1 hour.

3. To serve, dip the dariole moulds briefly into hot water to loosen the jellies, then turn out on to the plates. Accompany with the raspberry coulis and the remaining berries, if you like.

Tip > It is imperative that you allow the jelly to set properly between the addition of each layer of fruit.

Chocolate Tart
Tarte sablée au chocolat amer

Everyone loves chocolate and this tart is the perfect end to any meal. The chocolate you use here will dictate the smoothness and flavour of the end product, so buying the best you can find is very important. These quantities should yield a tart to serve 10. This was created by Roger Pizey, my pastry chef at Harvey's.

500 g best-quality dark chocolate (see Tip below), broken
   into smallish pieces
3 eggs
200 ml milk
350 ml double cream
1 x 20 cm Sweet Pastry Tart Case (page 180)

Garnish
chocolate shavings made using a potato peeler
icing sugar

1. Pre-heat the oven to 180°C.

2. Melt the chocolate in a bain marie (a bowl set over a pan of gently boiling water works very well here). Remove from the heat.

3. Whisk the eggs in a large bowl. Place the milk and cream in a saucepan and carefully bring to a gentle boil. Add to the eggs and whisk to combine. Pass the mixture through a sieve on to the chocolate and mix well.

4. Pour the chocolate filling into the tart case. Place the tart in the oven, close the door and immediately turn the oven off. Leave the tart inside for 45 minutes.

5. When cool, trim the edges of the pastry case and cut the tart into the number of portions required. Serve with chocolate shavings on the top and sprinkled with icing sugar.

Tip > I use Valhrona Equatorial chocolate and I suggest that you do too. Failing that, a chocolate with 70% cocoa solids will do.

Soufflé Rothschild with a Purée of Apricots 'Albert Roux'

Soufflé Rothschild, coulis d'abricot

A classic dessert, this was created by my old boss Albert Roux, who was like a father figure to me when I worked for him. He will always have a special place in my heart. This is an utterly sophisticated pudding – not for the faint-hearted, but the extra effort is well worth it.

8 tbsp Crème Pâtissière (page 182)

4 tbsp Cointreau

16 egg whites

400 g caster sugar

100 g unsalted butter, softened

Garnish

16 halves Poached Apricots (page 181)

240 ml Apricot Purée (page 181)

2 tsp Cointreau

1. Pre-heat the oven to 180°C.

2. Put the poached apricots and purée in two separate pans. Add the Cointreau to the purée. Just before serving, warm the apricots and purée gently.

3. Put the crème pâtissière and Cointreau into a bowl and whisk thoroughly together. Place the egg whites in another bowl and whisk to soft peaks, then gradually whisk in the sugar until the mixture is stiff.

4. Take a flat ovenproof pan about 40 cm in diameter and brush it thoroughly with some of the butter, up and over the sides. Place in the oven for 10 minutes to allow it to become red-hot.

5. Add one-quarter of the whisked egg white to the crème pâtissière and whisk together. Fold in the remaining egg white carefully.

6. Take the pan out of the oven and brush thoroughly with butter again. Delicately spoon the soufflé mixture into the pan and knock it lightly on the work surface to help it fall into place; the pan should be full. Cook briefly for 30 seconds on the hob, then place the pan in the oven to cook for 7 minutes until the soufflé is nicely browned.

7. To serve, pour the warm apricot purée on to a plate and arrange the poached apricots around the edge. Turn the soufflé out of the pan, smooth side up, on to the centre of the plate. Serve immediately.

Tip > Make the poached apricots and apricot purée in advance.

Caramelized Apple Tart with Caramel Sauce and Vanilla Ice Cream

Tarte fine aux pommes caramalisée, glace vanille

The combination of hot caramel, apples and ice cream makes for a lovely pudding, sort of refined comfort food. You could, of course, buy the vanilla ice cream, but go for a good brand made with vanilla beans and double cream. This dessert was invented by my pastry chef, Thierry Busset, at 'The Restaurant, Marco Pierre White'.

160 g Puff Pastry (page 179)

8 apples

2 tbsp caster sugar

60 g unsalted butter, melted

Caramel Sauce (page 185), warmed for serving

4 scoops Vanilla Ice Cream (page 183)

1. Pre-heat the oven to 180°C.

2. Divide the puff pastry into four equal portions and roll out each one very thinly to 8–10 cm in diameter. Prick the pastry all over with a fork to prevent it from rising during baking.

3. Place the four pieces of pastry on a baking sheet. Using a small side plate as a guide, trim the pastry to four neat discs. Turn over at the edges to give an even appearance.

4. Peel, core and halve the apples vertically, then slice them very, very thinly crossways. You will need a very sharp small knife to do this; a paring knife would be perfect. Fan out the slices carefully and neatly on the puff pastry discs, making a large circle with a smaller circle in the middle. Sprinkle with the sugar and pour over the melted butter evenly.

5. Bake for 20 minutes, then very carefully, using a fish slice, turn the tarts over. Bake apple side down for a further 10 minutes.

6. Take the tarts out of the oven and immediately press on them with the bottom of a pan to flatten them, then turn them right side up on individual plates.

7. To serve, put a scoop of cold ice cream in the middle of each tart and spoon the warm caramel sauce all around.

Shortcut > You can cheat a little by using ready made puff pastry. The secret is to roll it out very thinly.

Millefeuille of Red Fruits with Kirsch Sabayon

Millefeuille aux fruits rouges, sabayon de Kirsch

This is so pretty and very light and fresh. The pastry cases can be made in advance (you could cheat and use frozen puff pastry), then gently reheated whilst you prepare the sabayon, which has to be made at the very last minute.

200 g Puff Pastry (page 179)
sifted icing sugar to dust
Raspberry Coulis (page 182)
1 punnet each of raspberries, blackberries, blueberries and redcurrants
Sweet Sabayon (page 184) made with Kirsch

1. Pre-heat the oven to 220°C.

2. Roll out the puff pastry very thinly, to a thickness of 3 mm, then leave to rest in the fridge for an hour. Cut into eight 10 cm discs and put these back in the fridge to rest.

3. Place the pastry discs on a non-stick tray and dust with icing sugar. Bake for 15 minutes until golden brown and shiny on the top. They will rise like puffed-up little balls, with the sugar glazing their tops. Remove from the oven.

4. Choose the four neatest and best pastries for the tops of your millefeuilles. Cut a circle from the bottoms of these and very carefully remove any raw pastry from the inside, taking care not to damage the pastry cases. Do the same at the tops of the other four pastries. Place the tops on the bottoms so you have four double millefeuilles.

5. Put the raspberry coulis and red fruits in a saucepan, ready to heat. Then make the sabayon. A few minutes before it is finished, heat through the fruits very, very gently. They mustn't cook, just lightly warm through.

6. To serve, place a millefeuille in the centre of each plate. Remove the top and fill the bottom section with the fruit and juices, allowing them to spill over and around the edges of the plate. Spoon over the thick creamy sabayon and top with the glazed puff pastry tops.

Tart of Pear and Red Fruits, Poire Williams

Sablé de poires aux fruits rouges, sabayon de Poire Williams

I love cooking different fruits of varying textures together, and this fabulous and rather luxurious dessert is a perfect example of that. You can prepare most of the components well in advance, then assemble the dish on the day. The sabayon needs to be made at the very last minute, just before serving. This will serve six.

6 medium pears, peeled
700 g caster sugar
150 ml Poire Williams (pear eau de vie)
2 vanilla pods, split lengthways

Sablé biscuits
400 g unsalted butter, at room temperature
200 g caster sugar
1 egg yolk
500 g plain flour

Garnish
85 ml Raspberry Coulis (page 182), optional
1 punnet each of blackberries, blueberries, redcurrants and blackcurrants
Sweet Sabayon (page 184) flavoured with Poire Williams
sifted icing sugar
6 sprigs of mint

1. To make the pastry for the sablés, beat together the butter and sugar by hand in a bowl. Add the egg yolk and mix in lightly, then add the flour. Mix in with your fingers to a nice crumb texture. (The lighter the touch and the cooler your fingers, the better the end result will be.)

2. Place the mix on a work surface, marble if possible as this is nice and cool, and rub together, then roll into a ball, working as quickly as possible. Wrap in plastic film and leave to rest in the fridge for 12 hours.

3. Roll out the pastry to about 3 mm thick (i.e. very thin) and cut into rectangles of 7.5 cm x 5 cm. You need 18 for this dish. Place on a baking sheet and rest in the fridge for another hour.

4. Pre-heat the oven to 170°C.

5. Bake the sablés for 10–12 minutes until light brown. Take care not to overbrown, as the taste of the sablés changes dramatically the darker they become. Leave to cool.

6. To poach the pears, put the sugar and 1 litre of water in a pan and slowly bring to the boil. When the sugar has dissolved, add the Poire Williams and split vanilla pods. Put the pears into the syrup and poach until tender – they are ready when a thin knife blade meets only a little resistance in the centre. Take the pan off the heat and leave the pears to cool in the syrup. When completely cool, drain the pears, halve and core.

7. If you are using the raspberry coulis, gently roll the red fruits in it to glaze. Make the sweet sabayon, flavouring it with Poire Williams.

8. To serve, place a sablé biscuit in the centre of each plate and top with half a pear, sliced quite thinly and fanned out. Coat with a little sabayon. Repeat these layers, then top with a third sablé biscuit. Sprinkle with icing sugar and add a small amount of the red fruits and the mint sprigs. Arrange the remaining red fruits decoratively around the plate.

Tip > The pears need to be perfectly ripe. As so many of the pears we find in supermarkets these days are very hard, you should buy them a few days in advance and ripen them at home. I suggest keeping them in a brown paper bag in an airing cupboard.

Feuillantine of Fresh Raspberries
Feuillantine de framboises

This dessert never fails to make an impression, as it is really quite beautiful on the plate. Whilst there is next to no cooking involved, the pastry circles need to be razor thin and totally flat to insure that assembly is easy. You can make the components well in advance and assemble it as required.

700 g Puff Pastry (page 179)
sifted icing sugar
600 g raspberries
Raspberry Coulis (page 182)
4 sprigs of fresh mint
double cream (optional)

1. Roll out the puff pastry on a work surface sprinkled with icing sugar to a rectangle 3 mm thick. Carefully roll up the pastry like a Swiss roll, and chill in the fridge for 2 hours.

2. Pre-heat the oven to 200°C.

3. With a sharp knife, cut the pastry roll across into 1 cm slices. Roll out each slice until paper thin, then cut into discs using a plain 10 cm cutter. Place on a non-stick baking tray and bake for about 15 minutes until golden brown.

4. Remove from the oven and turn the discs over. Flatten them with a bang using the bottom of a small saucepan. Leave to cool.

5. To serve, build up layers on each plate: first pastry, then raspberries, then pastry again, then more raspberries, and finishing with a third disc of pastry. Dust the whole thing with icing sugar. Spoon the raspberry coulis around the plates and top each feuillantine with a couple of raspberries and a sprig of mint. If using, now is the time to drizzle the cream over the top, allowing it to cascade down the sides.

Tip > If the raspberries you are using are very fresh and of good quality you won't need to glaze them with the coulis, but if they are less than perfect I suggest that you do.

Chocolate Surprise
Cadeau de chocolat

This is just glorious, a rich chocolate sponge layered with dark and white chocolate mousses all wrapped inside a chocolate gift box. It never fails to cause a stir and is the ultimate pressie for the chocoholic. As ever you should only use the best possible quality ingredients. Quantities here will serve 12 – or six very greedy people. Serve with cream or cinnamon crème anglaise.

Chocolate sponge

6 eggs, separated

175 g caster sugar

165 g plain flour

100 g cornflour

25 g cocoa powder

300 ml syrup made from 150 ml water and 150 g caster sugar

2 tbsp dark rum

Dark chocolate mousse

400 g good dark chocolate, broken into small pieces

12 egg yolks

250 g caster sugar

150 ml espresso coffee

700 ml double cream, whipped until thick

White chocolate mousse

300 g good white chocolate, broken into small pieces

3 gelatine leaves

85 ml hot water

300 ml double cream, whipped until thick

Chocolate box

about 600 g good dark chocolate, broken into small pieces

1. Pre-heat the oven to 190°C.

2. To make the sponge, whisk together the egg yolks and 75 g of the caster sugar. In a separate bowl whisk the egg whites with the remaining 100 g caster sugar until stiff. Sift together the flour, cornflour and cocoa powder.

3. Pour the egg yolk mixture into the egg whites. Add the sifted dry ingredients slowly and fold the whole thing together, taking care to retain as much of the air in the egg whites as possible.

4. Spread the mixture carefully on a 60 cm x 40 cm non-stick baking tray. Bake for about 20 minutes. To test whether the sponge is ready gently poke the middle with a finger: the indentation should remain for a couple of seconds before bouncing back. Cool the sponge in the tray on a wire rack.

5. When the sponge is cool, moisten with the syrup mixed with the rum.

6. To make the dark chocolate mousse, melt the dark chocolate slowly in a bowl set over a pan of hot water; remove from the heat.

7. Place the egg yolks in a bowl and beat thoroughly, then set the bowl over a pan of hot water or a bain marie. Continue beating until thick and pale. Remove from the heat.

8. Dissolve the sugar in the espresso, then boil to a thin syrup. Pour this syrup on to the egg yolks, whisking continuously. Remove from the pan of hot water and whisk until cold. When cold, mix this sabayon with the melted chocolate and then the whipped cream. Leave to cool.

9. Spread the dark chocolate mousse over the moistened sponge base. Place in the fridge to set.

10. To make the white chocolate mousse, melt the chocolate slowly in a bowl set over a pan of hot water. Meanwhile, put the gelatine leaves in the 85 ml hot water and allow to soften and melt. Mix the gelatine with the melted chocolate. When cool, fold in the whipped cream.

11. Spread the white chocolate mousse evenly and smoothly over the set dark chocolate mousse. Bang the tray on the work surface to get rid of any air bubbles. Put the completed *pavé* in the fridge to set (this takes quite a long time).

12. To make the chocolate gift boxes, cut the *pavé* into 12 (or fewer) portions – say 15 cm in length. For each box, cut a strip of pliable plastic about 18 cm long by 10 cm wide.

13. Melt the dark chocolate gently in a bowl set over a pan of hot water; remove from the heat. Spread some of the melted dark chocolate on to one side of a plastic strip using a palette knife.

14. Gripping the strip with your fingertips on either side, lift it up and wrap it around one of the portions of *pavé*. Crimp it in slowly using your fingers at the top so that it comes over the top and wraps the *pavé* like a parcel. Place in the fridge to set.

15. Wrap the remaining portions of *pavé* in the same way, and refrigerate.

16. Once the chocolate has set, slowly and carefully peel off the plastic, using your fingernails. The plastic will come off in one piece and will leave a shimmer on the chocolate that looks almost metallic. You will now have chocolate-wrapped gift boxes of chocolate.

17. To serve, set a gift box in the centre of each plate and surround with cream or crème anglaise.

Tip > If you make your *pavé* of sponge and mousses a day in advance, all you have to do on the day is to 'gift wrap' each portion in chocolate.

The most poisonous sauce is a chef's ego.

Chapter Six
Basic Recipes

Stocks and Essences

Chicken Stock

Makes about 4.5 litres

2.75 kg raw chicken carcases, roughly chopped
3 celery sticks
1 leek
1 large onion
2 carrots
$^1/_2$ head of garlic

1. Place the chicken carcases in a large pot, cover with about 5.75 litres cold water and bring to the boil. Skim well.

2. Keep the vegetables whole but peel them if necessary. Tie the celery and leek together with string; this prevents them from breaking up, and helps to keep the stock clear. Add all the vegetables and garlic to the pot. Bring back to the boil, skimming, then simmer gently for 4 hours.

3. Pass through a fine sieve. The stock should be a light amber colour and clear. It can be stored in the fridge for a couple of days or frozen for up to 3 months.

Fish Stock

Makes about 2 litres

1.8 kg fish bones (turbot or Dover sole are best)
white of 1 small leek, finely chopped
1 large celery stick, finely chopped
$1/2$ onion, finely chopped
$1/2$ fennel bulb, finely chopped
$1/2$ head of garlic (cut horizontally)
1 tbsp olive oil
200 ml white wine
1 lemon, sliced
2 sprigs of parsley

1. Wash the fish bones very thoroughly and chop roughly.

2. Cook the vegetables and garlic in the oil for a few minutes to soften without colouring. Add the fish bones and white wine and cook for about 5 more minutes (the bones will turn white), then reduce the wine a little.

3. Add 2 litres water, bring to the boil and skim well. Add the sliced lemon and parsley, then simmer for 20 minutes.

4. Pass through a sieve and leave to cool. The stock can be stored in the fridge for a day only, or frozen for up to a month.

Veal Stock

This stock will give your sauces so much more body than when using a chicken stock, due to the high gelatine content in veal bones. Make in large quantities and freeze.

Makes about 3 litres

2.75 kg veal knuckle bones
120 ml olive oil
1 onion, chopped
3 carrots, chopped
3 celery sticks, chopped
$^{1}/_{2}$ head of garlic
4 tbsp tomato purée
450 g button mushrooms
$^{1}/_{2}$ bottle of Madeira
10 litres hot water
sprig of thyme
1 bay leaf

1. Cook the veal bones in 4 tablespoons of the olive oil until golden brown, stirring and turning occasionally.

2. Simultaneously, in a separate pan, cook the onion, carrots, celery and garlic in 2 tablespoons of the oil until soft, without colouring.

3. Add the tomato purée to the vegetables and stir in, then allow it all to cook gently and colour lightly. Be very careful not to burn the ingredients.

4. In another pan, colour the button mushrooms in the remaining oil, then deglaze with the Madeira. Boil to reduce down to almost nothing. Add the syrupy mushrooms to the rest of the vegetables.

5. When the veal bones are golden brown, place them in a large stock pot and cover with the hot water. Add the vegetables and herbs and bring back to the boil. Skim, then allow to simmer for 8–12 hours, topping up with water as required to keep the bones covered.

6. Pass through a fine sieve into another, preferably tall pan and boil to reduce by half. Cool, then store. This can be kept in the fridge for up to a week or frozen for 3 months.

Beef Stock

This is a fabulous rich stock that can easily be used as a consommé or as the base for a sauce for red meat dishes. It takes time and a little effort but it's worth it.

Makes about 1.5 litres

1 beef shin, sliced into 5 pieces

$1/_2$ calf's foot or pig's trotter

$1/_2$ large ox tongue

$1/_2$ boiling fowl

$1/_2$ onion

1 carrot

1 leek

10 button mushrooms, sliced

500 ml Madeira, simmered to reduce by one-quarter

200 ml soy sauce

1 tbsp tomato purée

3 cloves

10 g rock salt

20 black peppercorns

1. Put the beef shin in a large, tall pan with the calf's foot, tongue and boiling fowl. Place all the vegetables on top and add the reduced Madeira. Add all the other ingredients with just enough cold water to cover. Bring to the boil and simmer for 6–7 hours.

2. Strain the hot stock carefully through muslin. Skim off the fat and allow to cool. Store in the fridge for up to a week or 3 months in the freezer.

Vegetable Stock

This wonderfully fragrant yet delicate stock adds flavour without overpowering food.

Makes about 850 ml

2 courgettes

4 onions

1 fennel bulb

2 leeks

8 garlic cloves, crushed

14 black peppercorns

50 g butter

15 g each chervil, basil and tarragon, chopped

1. Roughly chop the vegetables, then sweat them with the garlic and peppercorns in the butter until the vegetables are soft.

2. Add just enough cold water to cover (about 1 litre) and bring to the boil. Skim and simmer for about 15 minutes.

3. Add the herbs and cook for a further 2 minutes only. Strain immediately and allow to cool. Keep in a covered bowl in the fridge for up to a week or in the freezer for 3 months.

Court-Bouillon for Seafood

Makes about 1.75 litres

2 onions

1 leek

2 celery sticks

5 carrots

1 head of garlic, cut horizontally in half

6 slices of lemon

8 white peppercorns, crushed

20 pink peppercorns

1 bay leaf

2 star anise

sprig each of parsley, coriander, tarragon, thyme and chervil

200 ml dry white wine

1. Roughly chop all the vegetables and place in a large pan with the garlic, lemon, peppercorns, bay leaf and anise. Add just enough cold water to cover (about 1.75 litres) and bring to the boil. Reduce the heat and simmer for 8 minutes.

2. Add the herbs and cook for a further 2 minutes only.

3. Remove from the heat and add the wine. Pour the mixture into a large bowl or jar, cover and leave to infuse for $1\frac{1}{2}$ days in the fridge.

4. Strain the stock through a muslin-lined sieve and discard all the solids. Store the stock in a tightly covered jar in the fridge for up to a week or in the freezer for 3 months.

Scallop Stock

A stock made from scallop trimmings always makes the best sauce for scallops. For a simple sauce, reduce 150 ml of stock per person by half, then add 1 tablespoon double cream, 1 teaspoon unsalted butter, a squeeze of lemon, and salt and pepper to taste, and mix with a hand blender.

Makes about 2 litres

1 carrot, finely chopped
1 celery stick, finely chopped
1 small leek, finely chopped
1 tbsp olive oil
18 scallop skirts
2 litres Fish Stock (page 139) or water
1 cinnamon stick
pared zest of 1 lemon

1. Cook the vegetables in the oil for a few minutes to soften without colouring. Add the scallop skirts and cook for a few more minutes, without colouring.

2. Pour in the fish stock, bring to the boil and skim. Add the cinnamon and lemon zest and cook for 20 minutes (no longer, or the cinnamon and lemon would turn bitter).

3. Pass through a muslin-lined sieve and leave to cool. The stock can be stored in the fridge for about a day or frozen for up to a month.

Madeira Jelly

This jelly is full of flavour. I know it seems like a lot, but it freezes well for later use. To make a Sauternes jelly for the Terrine of Foie Gras on page 34, just replace the Madeira with Sauternes.

Makes about 3 litres stock

1 shin of veal, chopped into osso bucco

1 shin of beef, cut similarly

1 boiling fowl, chopped into small joints

1 calf's foot, split

2 onions, halved

2 carrots, split lengthways

2 celery sticks

2 leeks

1 head of garlic, cut horizontally in half

1 bouquet garni

1 bottle of Madeira

500 ml soy sauce

1. Put all the meats into a large stock pot along with all the remaining ingredients. Pour in 10 litres of water and bring to the boil. Keep skimming off the greyish residue from the surface until the liquid is clear, then cook uncovered for $2^1/_2$ hours. To insure a clear stock, the liquid should barely simmer, so the heat should be very low. A heat diffuser is useful for this process.

2. Strain gently through muslin into another pan; the stock should be totally clear and amber in colour. It can now be used for a broth or consommé. It will not require seasoning due to the addition of the soy sauce.

3. To make a jelly for a parfait or terrine, reduce the strained stock by half by simmering gently. Leave to set in shallow trays, then either serve the jelly smooth or chop it finely and pipe or spoon on for decoration and an intense burst of flavour.

Lamb Stock

Makes 1.5 litres

2.5 kg raw lamb bones
2 tbsp vegetable oil
1 onion
1 celery stick
1 carrot
1 leek
$2^{1}/_{2}$ tbsp Tomato Fondue (page 163)
1 head of garlic, cloves separated and peeled
1.5 litres Veal Stock (page 140)
1 litre Chicken Stock (page 138)
1 bay leaf
sprig of thyme

1. Chop the lamb bones very finely, then fry them in 1 tablespoon of the oil in a heavy tray on top of the stove until golden brown. Drain well.

2. Peel or trim the vegetables as needed, then cut into a dice. Sweat in the remaining oil in a large pan, without colouring.

3. Add the tomato fondue and garlic cloves, and cook right down to a 'jam'. Add the lamb bones.

4. Bring the two stocks to the boil in a separate pan and pour over the bones to cover. Bring back to the boil and add 500 ml cold water. (This addition of cold liquid will coagulate the fat in the stock and it will rise to the top.) Skim off the fat thoroughly.

5. Add the bay leaf and thyme and cook the stock at a fast simmer for 1 hour, skimming regularly. It will reduce down.

6. Pass through a sieve, then through muslin six times to ensure that it is clear. Cool and store in the fridge for up to a week or freezer for a month. Use as a stock or sauce.

Jus Rôti

This sauce is virtually a concentrated essence of roast meat juices. It can be made with either lamb (as here), or with chicken if it is to be served with poultry or game birds. This is a wonderful accompaniment to Roast Suckling Pig (page 90).

Makes 8 portions

an average shoulder of lamb
olive oil
200 ml Chicken Stock (page 138)
200 ml Veal Stock (page 140)

1. Pre-heat the oven to 140°C.

2. Roast the lamb for $1\frac{1}{2}$ hours, using very little oil in the tray.

3. Remove from the oven and add the stocks and 200 ml water to the roasting tray. Bring quickly to the boil on the hob, then remove the lamb from the liquid. Place it on a wire rack over the roasting tin.

4. Wrap plastic film very tightly over the top of the lamb and squeeze hard to drain all the meat juices into the roasting tray. Keep squeezing until no more liquid is forthcoming.

5. Discard the meat – or feed to the dog or cat – because in removing all the juices you have also removed all the flavour. Reduce the liquid to concentrate the flavour. When cold the essence can be stored in the fridge for up to a week or for 3 months in the freezer.

Cold Savoury Sauces

Mayonnaise

Makes 4–6 portions

2 egg yolks
1 tbsp Dijon mustard
2 tbsp white wine vinegar
1 tsp salt
dash of Tabasco sauce
500 ml groundnut oil

1. Place the egg yolks, mustard, vinegar, salt and Tabasco in a bowl and mix together. Add the oil drop by drop to start with, constantly whisking so that the yolks absorb the oil. When about half the oil has been incorporated, you can start adding the remaining oil in slightly larger amounts, continually whisking.

2. Once all the oil has been added and the sauce is thick, creamy and just a little stiff, it is ready for use. The mayonnaise can be stored in the fridge, well covered, for up to a week.

Vinaigrette

Makes 400 ml

75 ml white wine vinegar
120 ml groundnut oil
200 ml olive oil
salt and freshly ground white pepper

1. Place the vinegar in a bowl and add a pinch each of salt and pepper. Stir to dissolve. Add the oils and whisk to an emulsion. Taste and adjust the seasoning, if necessary.

2. Store in a suitable container. This keeps well for up to a week, stored in the fridge – whisk or shake well before use.

Water Vinaigrette

A good dressing for salad leaves.

Makes 400 ml

50 ml red wine
50 ml sherry vinegar
250 ml groundnut oil
50 ml olive oil
salt and freshly ground white pepper

Make and store as for Vinaigrette (above).

Rouille

Makes about 300 ml

2 egg yolks
50 g cooked potato, puréed
1 hard-boiled egg yolk, sieved
2 pinches of saffron strands
2 garlic cloves, crushed
200 ml olive oil
salt

1. Place the egg yolks, potato, hard-boiled egg yolk, saffron and garlic in a bowl and mix together.

2. Add the oil slowly as for a mayonnaise, whisking constantly. When all the oil has been incorporated and the sauce is thick, taste and season with salt.

Sauce Vierge

A wonderful and versatile sauce, great with fish and shellfish.

Makes 4 portions

85 ml olive oil
25 ml lemon juice
1 tsp coriander seeds, crushed
8 basil leaves, cut into fine julienne strips
2 tomatoes, skinned, seeded and diced

1. Heat the oil gently in a small pan, then add the lemon juice. Remove from the heat.

2. Add the coriander and basil and leave to infuse in the warm oil for few minutes.

3. Add the tomato dice and serve immediately.

Tomato Coulis

Makes 4 portions

200 g good-quality ripe tomatoes, roughly chopped
50 ml red wine vinegar
40 g tomato purée
dash each of tomato ketchup and Tabasco sauce
50 ml virgin olive oil
salt and freshly ground white pepper

1. Place all the ingredients except the oil in a food processor and blend to a purée. Add the oil and blend for 30 seconds.

2. Pass three times through a fine sieve to make a very smooth coulis. Taste and adjust the seasoning.

Sauce Gribiche

Makes 4 portions

2 hard-boiled eggs
capers
small gherkins (cornichons)
$^1/_2$ tsp chopped tarragon
1 $^1/_2$ tbsp chopped parsley
2 tbsp olive oil, or a little more

1. Weigh the eggs, out of their shells, then measure out the same weight of both capers and gherkins.

2. Separate the egg yolks from the whites; sieve the yolks and finely chop the whites. Chop the capers and gherkins. Mix all together in a bowl.

3. Add the herbs to the bowl, then gradually mix in enough oil just to bind. You may need a little more oil – the texture should be a firmish paste, not runny. Season to taste.

Tapenade

I often use this in fish sauces (see below), but it's also really good on warm toast.

Makes 8 portions

250 g good black olives, stoned
50 g anchovies
25 g capers, drained
$1^1/_2$ garlic cloves
2 tbsp olive oil

1. Place all the ingredients, except the olive oil, in a blender. Blend for about 5 minutes, then add the oil and blend briefly.

2. Decant into small, clean jars with screwtops. The tapenade can be stored in the fridge for up to 3 months.

Tapenade Sauce

To each 50–85 ml portion of Velouté for Fish (page 159), mix in 1 tablespoon Tapenade and finish with 15 g unsalted butter.

Hot Savoury Sauces

Tomato Sauce

Makes 4 portions

25 ml goose fat
50 g diced carrot
50 g diced onion
2 garlic cloves, crushed
40 g plain flour
2 thin slices of Parma ham, chopped
400 g plum tomatoes, skinned, seeded and chopped
50 g unsalted butter
salt and freshly ground white pepper

1. Heat the goose fat in a pan and soften the carrot, onion and garlic for a few minutes, without colouring. Stir in the flour and cook gently for 15–20 minutes.

2. Add the ham and tomatoes to the pan and bring to the boil. Season to taste. Cover and cook gently for 3 minutes.

3. Blend the sauce in a liquidizer, then push through a fine sieve. Heat gently without boiling, and add the butter to give the sauce a gloss.

Red Wine Sauce

The reductions for this basic red wine sauce can be prepared in advance. It can then be finished with the butter at the last moment. It is good served with eggs, fish, poultry, meat or game. Use a stock appropriate to the main ingredient – fish stock for fish, chicken stock for poultry/game, etc.

Makes 4 portions

500 ml good red wine
100 ml port
500 ml chosen stock (see above)
50 g chilled unsalted butter, diced

1. Pour the red wine and port into a suitable saucepan and boil to reduce by one-third.

2. In another pan, boil the stock to reduce it to a good coating consistency – it should lightly coat the back of a wooden spoon.

3. Add the red wine and port reduction, then add the butter dice and allow it to melt.

Sabayon of Grain Mustard

Makes 4 portions

400 ml Velouté for Fish (page 159)
4 egg yolks
4 tbsp clarified butter
4 tsp double cream, whipped
2 tsp grain mustard

1. Reduce the velouté by half and allow to cool slightly.

2. Meanwhile, gently beat the egg yolks with a few drops of water in a bowl over a bain marie or pan of hot water. As the egg yolks thicken smoothly, add the warm clarified butter, then remove from the heat.

3. Add the thickened egg mixture to the velouté together with the whipped cream and mustard. The texture should be thick but still pourable. Serve immediately.

Sauce Albuféra

Makes 2 portions

400 ml Chicken Stock (page 138)
400 ml double cream
150 g Foie Gras Butter (page 166)
salt and freshly ground white pepper

1. Place the stock in a pan and boil to reduce by one-third.

2. Add the cream, bring back to the boil and cook for a few minutes until the sauce thickens enough to coat the back of a spoon.

3. Remove from the heat and add the foie gras butter, allowing it to melt gently. Season with salt and pepper, then serve.

Velouté for Fish

The basic cream sauce for fish is best made on the day of serving.

Makes 4 portions

6 shallots, thinly sliced
15 g unsalted butter
500 ml white wine
500 ml Noilly Prat
1 litre Fish Stock (page 139)
1 litre double cream

1. Cook the shallots in the butter until softened, without colouring. Deglaze the pan with the white wine and Noilly Prat and boil to reduce to a syrup.

2. Add the fish stock and boil to reduce by half. Add the cream, bring back to the boil and simmer for 5 minutes to reduce to a coating consistency.

3. Pass through a fine sieve. Keep in the fridge, covered with plastic film, if not using immediately; reheat gently for serving.

Sauce Bercy

This is excellent with calf's liver (see page 105) and also with fillet or entrecote of beef.

Makes 4 portions

10 shallots, finely sliced into rings
150 ml port
500 ml red wine
300 ml Veal Stock (page 140)
10 g unsalted butter
1 tsp double cream
salt and freshly ground pepper

1. Marinate the shallots in the port for 24 hours, then cook in the port until soft. Leave to cool, then strain the port into another pan. Reserve the shallots.

2. Add the red wine to the port and boil to reduce by four-fifths (down to about 130 ml). Pour in the veal stock and boil to reduce to a good sauce consistency.

3. Add the cooked shallots, then whisk in the butter and cream. Taste and correct the seasoning.

Sauce Lie de Vin

This is really wonderful with fish, in particular salmon, turbot, brill or sea bass. Add the cream at the last minute.

Makes 4 portions

2 shallots, finely sliced
160 g unsalted butter
650 ml red wine
85 ml ruby port
250 ml Fish Stock (page 139)
250 ml Veal Stock (page 140)
$^1/_2$ star anise
50 ml double cream
salt and freshly ground white pepper

1. Sweat the shallots in 15 g of the butter until softened, without colouring. Add the wine and port and boil to reduce by two-thirds.

2. In another pan boil the fish and veal stocks together with the star anise to reduce by half.

3. Add the stock reduction to the wine reduction. Boil together for 5 minutes, then pass through a muslin cloth into yet another pan.

4. Add the cream and return to the heat. Dice the remaining butter and whisk into the sauce. Season to taste.

Sauce Nero

This black sauce is served with seafood.

Makes 4 portions

2 shallots, sliced
25 g unsalted butter
200 ml white wine
200 ml Fish Stock (page 139)
200 ml double cream
50 ml squid ink
salt and freshly ground white pepper

1. Sweat the shallots in the butter until soft, without colouring. Add the wine and boil to reduce by half. Add the stock and again reduce by half.

2. Add the cream and cook for a further 5 minutes.

3. Season to taste, then add the squid ink to create a velvety black sauce. Pass through a fine sieve.

Tomato Fondue

This is a very thick, fresh tomato sauce that is very useful in quite a number of dishes. You can make it a couple of days before you need it.

Makes about 150 ml

100 ml olive oil
$1/2$ shallot, finely chopped
1 garlic clove, finely chopped
6–8 large, very ripe plum tomatoes, skinned, seeded and diced
sprig of thyme
$1/4$ bay leaf

1. Heat the olive oil in a pan and sweat the shallot and garlic for a few minutes without colouring. Add the tomato dice and herbs. Cook very gently until all the moisture has been removed from the tomato and you are left with a dry paste.

2. Remove the herbs and put the mixture in a blender. Blend until smooth.

Savoury Preparations

Chicken Mousse

Makes about 450 g

200 g skinless boneless chicken breast, sinews removed and chopped
pinch of ground mace
1 tbsp chopped tarragon
1 egg
2 tsp salt
225 ml double cream

1. Process the chicken with the mace and tarragon in a blender for 1 minute until smooth. Add the egg and salt, and process the mixture for another minute. Chill the mixture for 10–15 minutes (this will prevent it from separating later).

2. Add the cream, then force the mixture through a sieve to make a velvety texture. Taste and adjust the seasoning.

3. Store the mousse wrapped in plastic film in the fridge until needed.

Soft Herb Crust

A great topping for fish. Use white breadcrumbs, preferably brioche.

Makes 8 portions

175 g fresh breadcrumbs
80 g Gruyère cheese, grated
50 g parsley, chopped
5 g thyme, chopped
125 g unsalted butter, at room temperature
salt and freshly ground white pepper

1. Place all the ingredients in a food processor and process until thoroughly mixed.

2. Spread out on a tray lined with greaseproof paper and open-freeze. Package in smaller quantities and store in the freezer for up to 3 months. Thaw before using.

Mushroom Duxelles

Makes about 50 g

225 g button mushrooms
1 tbsp whipping cream
salt and freshly ground pepper

1. Wipe the mushrooms and trim the stalks if necessary. Chop very finely in a food processor or by hand.

2. Heat the mushrooms in a dry pan until their liquid comes out and evaporates. The mushrooms will wilt and shrink.

3. Add the cream and stir in to blend with the mushrooms. Season to taste.

Foie Gras Butter

Makes 150 g

75 g cooked foie gras
75 g unsalted butter

1. Have the cooked foie gras and the butter at room temperature so they are the same consistency. Either put them into a food processor, blend together and push through a fine sieve, or sieve the foie gras on its own and then whisk in the butter.

2. Form into a suitable shape or shapes, such as little blocks, and then either refrigerate or freeze. The butter can be kept in the fridge for up to a week.

Savoury Garnishes

Ratatouille

This is drier than a normal ratatouille, which is very useful when using it as a garnish.

Makes 4 small portions

4 peppers (2 red and 2 yellow)
2 large courgettes
1 small aubergine
olive oil
1 small onion, finely diced
25 g Tomato Fondue (page 163)
6 basil leaves, cut into thin strips
1 plum tomato, skinned, seeded and diced
salt and freshly ground white pepper

1. Skin and seed the peppers, then cut them into a small dice. Cut the skin with a little flesh from the courgettes and aubergine – about 5 mm thick – and dice this (use the remaining flesh in another dish).

2. Heat a little olive oil in a large pan and cook the pepper dice gently for a few minutes. It should still be crisp and bright in colour. Remove with a slotted spoon to a plate.

3. Cook the courgette, aubergine and onion dice separately in the same pan, using a little more olive oil each time. They too should remain bright and crisp. Remove with the slotted spoon to a plate.

4. Heat the tomato fondue gently in a thick-based pan. Add the basil and cook for 1 minute.

5. Add all the vegetable dice, including the tomato, and mix together over a gentle heat. Season to taste. If not using immediately, reheat for serving.

Sauté Potatoes

Makes 4 portions

4 large baking potatoes
salt
goose fat

1. Cook the potatoes, in their skins, in boiling salted water until two-thirds done. Drain and allow to cool before peeling.

2. Cut each potato into five slices, then use a cutter to make them neat and uniform in size.

3. Fry in goose fat until tender and golden brown. Drain well and serve as soon as you can.

Basic Mashed Potato

Makes 4–6 portions

1 kg Desirée potatoes
8 g ($^1/_2$ tbsp) salt
200 g unsalted butter
90 ml double cream

1. Peel the potatoes and cut into 2.5 cm cubes.

2. Put 1 litre water in a pan, add the potatoes and salt and bring to the boil. Poach the potatoes for 4–5 minutes. Drain well and pat dry with kitchen paper.

3. Purée the potatoes in a food processor, then add the butter and cream. Serve hot.

Pommes Purée

You can make this in advance, in the morning of the day you need it. If doing this, beat in 75 g of the butter, then cool and keep in the fridge. Before serving, warm the purée and beat in the remaining butter.

Makes 4 portions

4 large potatoes, peeled
100 g unsalted butter
salt and freshly ground white pepper

1. Put the potatoes in a large saucepan and cover with cold water. Add 1 teaspoon salt, bring to the boil and simmer until tender.

2. Drain the potatoes. Purée in a vegetable mill (mouli-légumes), then pass through a fine sieve.

3. Beat in the butter, season to taste and serve.

Buttered Cabbage

Makes 4 portions

1 Savoy cabbage
100 g clarified butter
salt and freshly ground white pepper

1. Cut the cabbage in half. Remove and discard the stalk and core, and shred the leaves finely. Blanch in boiling salted water for 1 minute only, then drain.

2. Heat the clarified butter in a large frying pan and toss the cabbage in this for 1 minute until just tender but still a little crisp. Season with salt and pepper and serve hot.

Confit of Fennel

Baby fennel is perfect for this, but if you can't find them sliced larger bulbs can be used.

Makes 4 portions

8 baby fennel bulbs
14 black olives, halved and stoned
50 ml olive oil
salt

1. Trim the fennel bulbs, leaving 1 cm of the stalks (or trim and slice 1 or 2 medium bulbs). Blanch in boiling salted water for 3 minutes, then drain and refresh in iced water. Drain and dry.

2. Before serving, heat the fennel through with the olives in the olive oil until tender. This will take about 2 minutes, depending on size.

Confit of Garlic

Makes 4 portions

goose fat
12–16 large garlic cloves, unpeeled
2 bay leaves
2 small sprigs of thyme

1. Half fill a small pan with goose fat and heat to 90°C.

2. Add the garlic cloves, bay leaves and thyme. Heat until the fat is about 80°C. Cook at this temperature for 20–30 minutes until the garlic is tender to the touch. Remove from the heat and allow the garlic to cool in the fat. Once cold, store in the goose fat in the fridge.

3. To serve, remove the garlic cloves from thc fat and fry in a dry pan to crisp up.

Aubergine Tians

This interesting garnish goes well with lamb or fish.

Makes 4 portions

1 medium aubergine
olive oil
4 tbsp Tomato Fondue (page 163), warmed for serving
4 sun-dried tomatoes, sliced
flaked sea salt (*fleur de sel*)

1. Cut the aubergine across into four 3.75 cm slices. Prick the flesh with a fork.

2. Shallow fry the aubergine slices in olive oil until evenly cooked and slightly soft. Drain well on kitchen paper.

3. Cover the top of each slice of aubergine with tomato fondue and arrange slices of sun-dried tomato on this. Sprinkle with flaked sea salt and serve hot.

Sage Beignets

This is perfect with red mullet or other grilled fish. The beignets could also be served as a canapé.

Makes 4 portions

16 large sage leaves
1 tbsp Tapenade (page 154)
olive oil

Batter
250 ml beer (Belgian lager makes for a very light batter)
25 g fresh yeast
200 g plain flour
pinch of salt

1. For the batter, gently warm a little of the beer on the hob to room temperature. Off the heat, cream the yeast with the warm beer, then add the rest of the beer.

2. Sift the flour and salt into a bowl and make a well in the centre. Slowly pour in the beer and yeast mixture, whisking until all has been incorporated. The batter should be quite runny. Leave to stand for about 3 hours to allow it to activate.

3. Sandwich pairs of sage leaves together with a little tapenade. Make eight sandwiches, so there are two per portion.

4. Heat some olive oil in a pan. Dip the sage leaves in the batter, then shallow fry in the hot oil until light and crisp. Drain on kitchen paper and serve immediately.

Parsnip Purée

This can be made a few hours in advance. Add 100 g of the butter and then, before serving, add the rest of the butter and warm through gently.

Makes 4 portions

450 g parsnips
1 small potato
450 ml milk
120 g unsalted butter
salt

1. Peel and chop the parsnips and potato and put into a saucepan. Cover with the milk and 150 ml water, and add a large pinch of salt. Cook until really soft.

2. Drain in a colander, then press to remove excess moisture. Pass through a vegetable mill (mouli-légumes) and then through a fine sieve.

3. Add the butter and salt to taste. Mix together and serve immediately

Garniture Bourguignonne

All three elements of this garnish can be prepared in advance, then reheated individually for serving. The onions keep extremely well in the stock, which will set to a jelly. Use this garnish for the beef daube on page 88.

Makes 4 portions

200 g small button mushrooms
20 g unsalted butter
200 g smoked bacon, rinded and cut into thin lardons
vegetable oil
200 g sliverskin onions, peeled
Veal Stock (page 140) to cover
salt and freshly ground white pepper

1. Sweat the mushrooms in the butter until tender. Drain well and season.

2. Cook the bacon lardons in a little oil in a non-stick pan until crisp. Drain.

3. Cook the onions in the veal stock until soft, then drain.

4. Just before serving, sprinkle the mushrooms, bacon and onions over each portion of the dish you are garnishing.

Etuvée of Chicory

Makes 2 portions

2 large heads chicory
75 g unsalted butter or 3 tbsp olive oil
Chicken Stock (page 138) to cover
salt and freshly ground black pepper

1. Remove any discoloured outer leaves from the chicory and cut off any green at the top. Cut off the root end. Divide each head lengthways into thirds or quarters, depending on the size.

2. Put the butter or oil in a large pan and gently sweat the pieces of chicory for a few minutes, without allowing them to colour.

3. Add stock to barely cover and continue to cook on a high heat until the stock and butter have virtually evaporated to a beautiful glaze and the vegetables are perfectly cooked and tender. Season to taste and serve immediately.

Roast Button Onions

Makes 4 portions

24 button onions
50 g butter
salt and freshly ground pepper

1. Pre-heat the oven to 220°C.

2. Top and tail the onions. Blanch in boiling salted water for 3 minutes. Drain and refresh in cold water, then pop the onions out of their skins.

3. Melt the butter in small, heavy-bottomed, flameproof pan over a moderate heat and add the onions and seasoning. Sauté for 3 minutes. Cover with buttered paper, put into the oven and roast for 5 minutes until the onions caramelize. Serve hot.

Pasta and Pastry

Fresh Pasta

Makes 600 g

600 g plain white flour
4 eggs
6 egg yolks
2 tbsp olive oil
pinch of salt

1. Place the flour in a food processor and switch the machine on. Slowly add the eggs and egg yolks through the feed tube, using the pulse button to mix.

2. When all the egg has been incorporated, add the olive oil and salt and mix in briefly.

3. Remove the pasta dough from the machine and knead for a few minutes on a lightly floured surface. Cover with plastic film and allow to rest for at least an hour before rolling and cutting as appropriate. The pasta dough can be frozen for later use.

Puff Pastry

Makes 1.1 kg

450 g strong plain flour
1 tsp salt
450 g unsalted butter, softened slightly
2 tsp white wine vinegar

1. Sift the flour into a mound on your work surface. Make a well in the middle and add the salt, 60 g of the butter, 180 ml water and the vinegar. Mix and knead until the dough is smooth and elastic. Mould the dough into a ball and score a cross across the top with a knife. Cover the dough with a cloth and leave to rest in a cool place for about an hour.

2. On a lightly floured surface, roll out the dough into a sheet about 20 cm square, rolling the corners a little more thinly than the centre.

3. Place the remaining butter in a block in the centre of the dough. Bring up the four corners of pastry over the butter to make an envelope.

4. Roll this out into a rectangle about 25 cm x 15 cm. Fold in three and turn by 90 degrees. This constitutes a 'turn'.

5. With the rolling pin at right angles to the folds, roll out again to a rectangle the same size as before. Fold in three as before and again turn the pastry by 90 degrees (in the same direction as previously). Two 'turns' have now been completed. Cover the dough and leave to rest in the fridge for an hour.

6. Repeat the procedure to complete two more 'turns', then rest the dough in the fridge for another hour.

7. Make two more 'turns'. A total of six 'turns' have now been completed. Rest the dough for 1 more hour in the fridge, after which it is ready for use. The dough will keep in the fridge for a day or two and also freezes well.

Sweet Tart Pastry

This is the pastry to use for sweet tarts. You will need roughly half of this – 500 g – per tart (see below). The pastry freezes well but make sure you wrap it carefully.

Makes 1 kg

700 g unsalted butter
300 g icing sugar
8 egg yolks
100 ml water
1 kg plain flour

1. Cream the butter and sifted icing sugar together in an electric mixer bowl until soft and white.

2. Add the egg yolks and beat in thoroughly. Turn the machine off and scrape the sides down into the mixture to make sure everything is incorporated. Beat again.

3. Add a little of the water, then add the flour and mix together thoroughly. Stop the machine every now and then to scrape down the sides. Add the remaining water and mix for 2–3 minutes.

4. Remove the pastry, wrap in plastic film and chill for at least 1 hour before using.

Sweet Pastry Tart Case

1. Roll out 500 g of pastry to 5 mm thick and use to line a 20 cm flan ring set on a baking sheet or a tart tin with a removable base. The ring should be 3.75 cm deep. Do not cut excess pastry off the top at this point. Rest for at least an hour in the fridge, to insure the pastry does not shrink during baking.

2. Pre-heat the oven to 180°C. Line the pastry case with greaseproof paper or foil and fill with baking beans. Bake blind for 15 minutes.

3. Remove from the oven and remove the foil or paper and the beans. Leave the pastry case to settle for a minute or two, then bake for a further 5 minutes until nice and golden. Allow to cool in the ring or tin before filling (and baking again if necessary). Trim the excess pastry before serving.

Sweets and Sweet Preparations

Poached Apricots

Makes 4 portions

900 g fresh apricots
2 vanilla pods

Poaching syrup
300 g caster sugar
50 ml Cointreau

1. To make the poaching syrup dissolve the sugar in 500 ml water and bring slowly to the boil. Make sure the sugar is completely dissolved.

2. Halve the apricots and place in another pan. Cover with the syrup and add the Cointreau. Split the vanilla pods, scrape the seeds into the pan and add the pods as well.

3. Bring to the boil, then immediately remove from the heat. Leave the apricots to cool in the syrup. They will be firm and delicious.

Apricot Purée

Cook the apricots as above, but simmer until they are really tender. Drain, reserving the syrup; remove the vanilla pods. Purée the apricots, then pass through a small sieve. The purée will be quite thick, studded with black vanilla seeds. If you need to thin it down, you can use some of the syrup. Serve with Soufflé Rothschild (page 124) or use as a sauce with vanilla ice cream.

Raspberry Coulis

Makes 4 portions

225 g raspberries
75 g icing sugar

1. Place the raspberries in a bowl and cover with the sugar. Leave for a while until the fruit juices start to flow.

2. Purée the mixture, then pass through a fine sieve to remove all the pips. Chill before serving.

Crème Pâtissière

This is normally used as a soufflé or sweet sauce base, but it could also be the filling for a tart. Make a day in advance so it has time to chill and set.

Makes 6 portions

3 egg yolks
35 g caster sugar
25 g plain flour
200 ml milk
50 ml lemon juice
finely grated zest of 2 lemons

1. In a pan cream the egg yolks and sugar together well, then mix in the flour.

2. Bring the milk and lemon juice and zest to the boil in another pan, then pour a little into the egg yolk mixture, whisking until smooth.

3. Add the remainder of the liquid and cook over a gentle heat for no longer than 5 minutes, stirring to a smooth cream.

Vanilla Ice Cream

Makes 10 portions

6 egg yolks
120 g caster sugar
500 ml milk
6 vanilla pods, split open
200 ml double cream

1. Beat together the eggs and the sugar in a bowl.

2. Put the milk in a pan. Scrape the seeds from the vanilla pods into the milk and add the pods too. Bring to the boil.

3. Pour the hot milk over the yolk mixture and mix well. Return the mixture to the pan and to the heat and cook very slowly, stirring, until the mixture thickens enough to coat the back of your spoon. This is basically a very highly flavoured crème anglaise.

4. Remove from the heat and pass through a fine sieve into a bowl set over ice, to cool the mixture down quickly.

5. When cold, whisk in the whipped cream. Put into an ice cream machine and churn until set and frozen.

Sweet Sabayon

This delicious sauce must be made just before serving. Choose an alcohol that complements the dish – Calvados for an apple dish, Kirsch for cherry, Framboise for raspberry, Poire Williams for pear and so on.

Makes 4 portions

100 g caster sugar
2 egg yolks
100 ml alcohol of choice (see above)

1. Dissolve the sugar in 100 ml water, then bring to the boil and cook to a slightly thickened syrup.

2. Place the egg yolks, syrup and alcohol in a wide, shallow pan and whisk together. Set over a gentle heat and continue to whisk until a foam starts to form.

3. Continue cooking very gently, whisking all the time, for at least 15 minutes until the sabayon is very light and fluffy.

Caramel Sauce

Makes 4 portions

60 g caster sugar
125 ml double cream

1. Melt the sugar gently in a heavy-based saucepan, then cook just as gently, without stirring, until you have a dark caramel.
2. Add the cream (very carefully as the hot caramel will make it boil and spit) and stir the two together to a sauce consistency. Serve warm. You can make the sauce up to 2 days in advance and keep it in the fridge.

Stock Syrup

Makes about 425 ml

225 g caster sugar

1. Dissolve the sugar in 300 ml water by slowly bringing to the boil, stirring to insure all the sugar dissolves. Continue to boil the syrup for 1 minute.
2. Pass through a sieve and cool, then store in a tightly covered jar in a cool place.

Never give a chef an office. He'll sit in it and stop working.

Index

AUTHOR'S ACKNOWLEDGEMENTS

I would like to give special thanks to Alexandra Antonioni for all her hard work and for delivering this book on time. I would also like to thank my chefs, Roger, Callum, Tim and Matthew, for all their hard work, and Natalka Znak, Richard Cowles, Beth Hart, Katie Rawcliffe, Jeanette Moffat, John Hollywood, Jane Beacon and Maria Knibbs at ITV who are working on Hell's Kitchen. Finally, I would like to congratulate all those at Ebury who worked so hard to make the book happen, especially Carey and Norma, who worked hand in hand with myself and Alex to get it produced in double quick time.

PHOTOGRAPHY CREDITS

Food photography by: **Sian Irvine** p25, p37, p39, p43, p47, p49, p69, p73, p77, p79, p83, p95, p99, p111, p115, p117, p121;
Norman Hollands p29, p33, p57, p63, p85, p91, p103, p123, p127, p129, p132; and **William Lingwood** p15.
Reportage and portraits by **Dave Bentley** p2, p4, p5, p6, p10, p12, p13, p22, p23, p52, p53, p80, p81, p108, p109, p136, p137, p186, p187, p192.